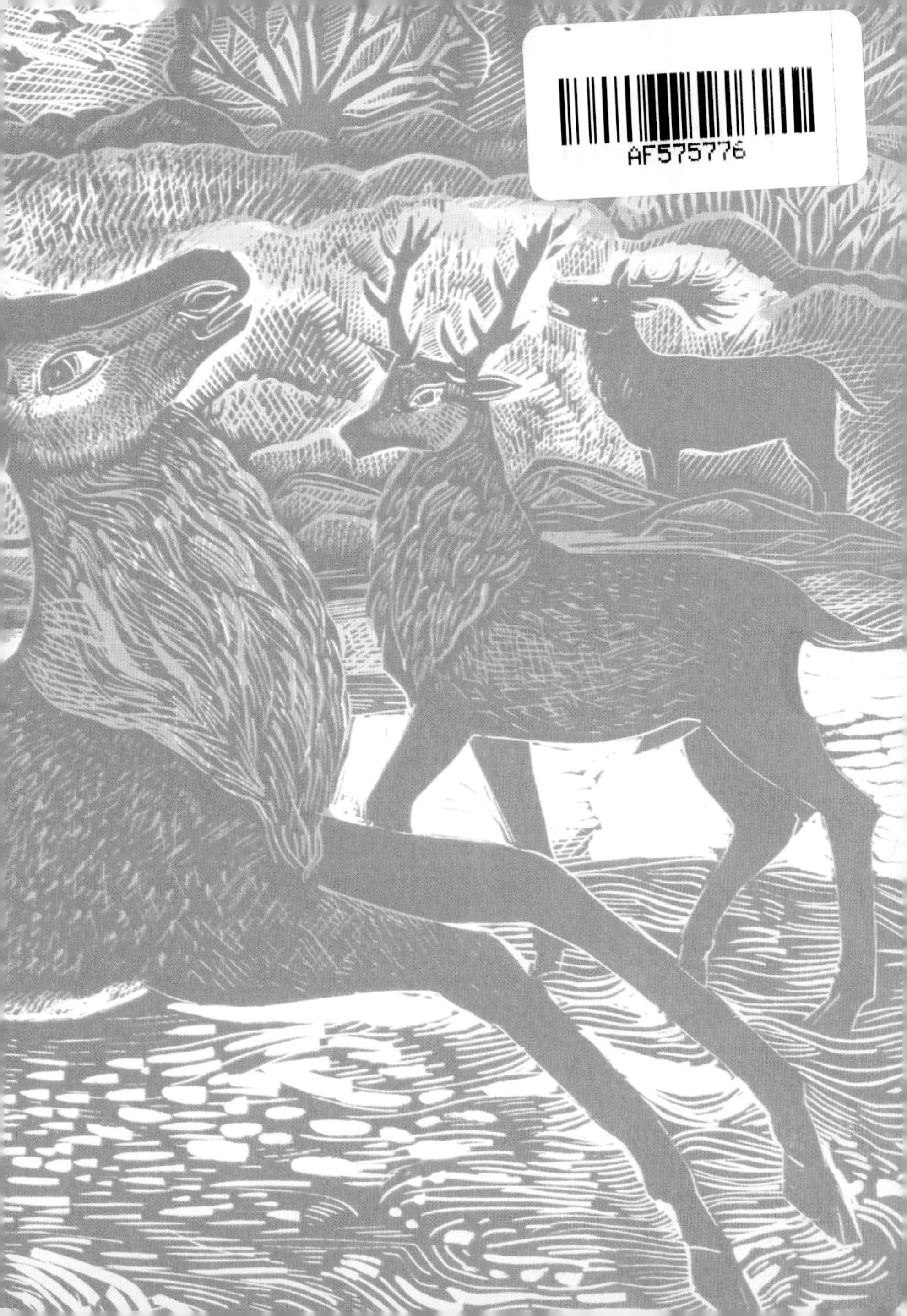

FALLING INTO AUTUMN

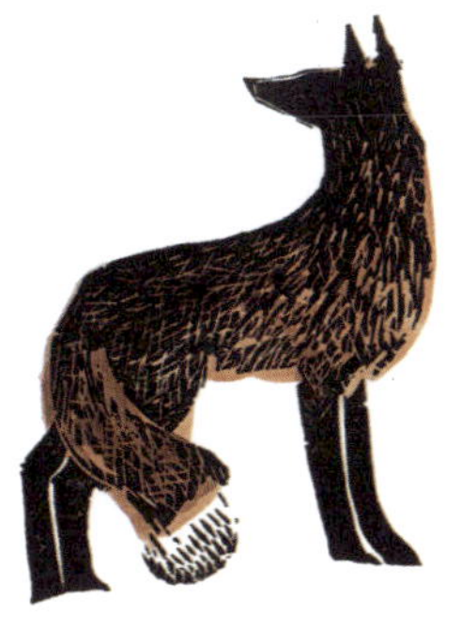

FALLING INTO AUTUMN

ANGELA HARDING

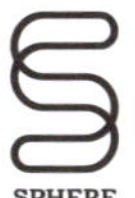

SPHERE

SPHERE

First published in Great Britain in 2025 by Sphere
1 3 5 7 9 10 8 6 4 2

A CIP catalogue for this book is available from the British Library.

ISBN 9781408721957

Project Editor: Helen Brocklehurst
Production Manager: Abby Marshall
Cover and interior design: Ben Prior
Typeset in Spectral Light
Printed in Italy by Printer Trento Srl
Papers used by Sphere are from well-managed forests and other responsible sources.

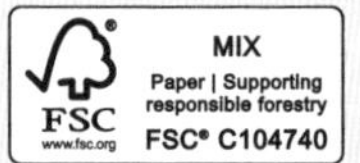

Sphere
An imprint of
Little, Brown Book Group
Carmelite House
50 Victoria Embankment
London EC4Y 0DZ

The authorised representative
in the EEA is
Hachette Ireland
8 Castlecourt Centre
Dublin 15, D15 XTP3, Ireland
(email: info@hbgi.ie)

An Hachette UK Company
www.hachette.co.uk
www.littlebrown.co.uk

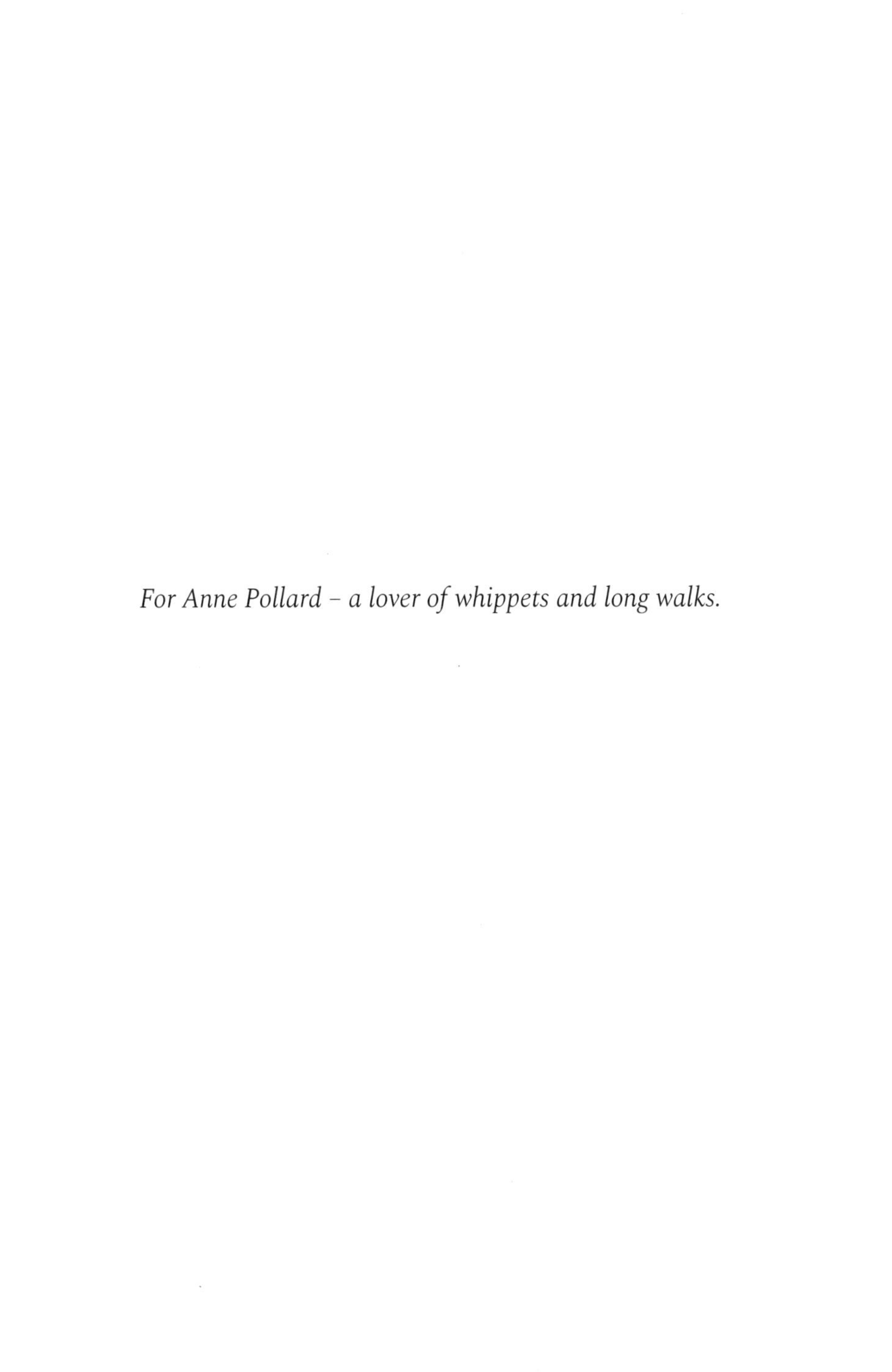

For Anne Pollard – a lover of whippets and long walks.

Introduction

Early autumn is when my husband, Mark, and I enjoy the last days of sailing before the boat must be put away for the winter. *Windsong* is a small clinker-built boat, which means she spends the winter in the water, with the top part of the boat well wrapped against the elements. But before that, she takes us to some beautiful places. One of these is the Butley River in Suffolk. The Butley is not far from *Windsong*'s winter mooring in Martlesham Creek, so it is a regular place to visit in the autumn. We moor the boat on a buoy in the middle of the river. This gives us a fantastic vantage point to watch the plentiful wildlife.

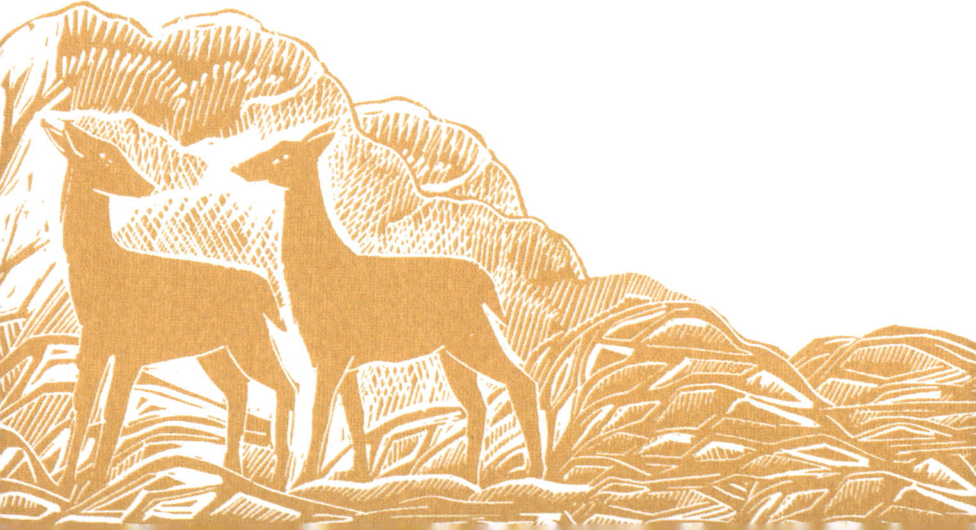

Our mooring place is close to a small jetty, which is used by a kingfisher as a fishing post. Every morning and evening, the kingfisher returns to this same post; the bird is a whirling, beautiful flash of orange and turquoise. We also watch seals basking on the riverbank, waiting for the tide to turn and bring them a fishy supper. On each side of the river are grassy fields – feeding places for flocks of autumn geese. Canada, greylag, pink-footed and barnacle geese spend the day there. But in the evening, they move further inland to their night-time roosts. Moving from these fields is not done quietly. The geese start with one or two honking calls, but before long the calls build to a deafening crescendo. We sit aboard *Windsong*, beer in hand, watching great honking clouds of geese skim over the boat. The flocks have to part round our mast, then rejoin into one big whirling mass of feathers and noise. It is a spellbinding moment. Once the light has gone, the geese are gone, and the river is still and quiet.

Autumn at home is a great time for woodland walks. We live in Rutland, which still has some deciduous woods.

Opposite:
Night Fox
(Linocut and silkscreen)

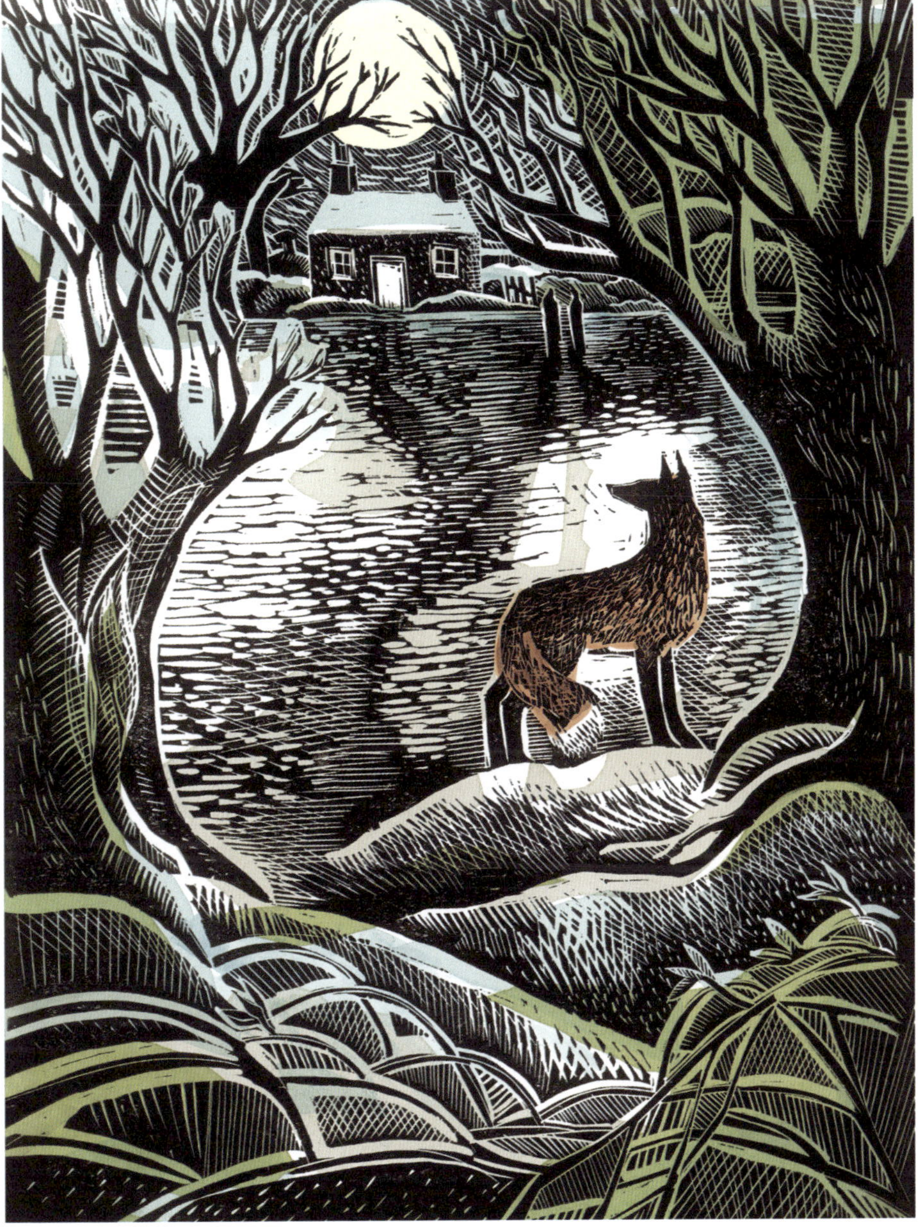

These woods are home to owls, jays, woodpeckers and deer. I have been very lucky to watch these not only in the woodland close to my home, but at the Knepp Estate in Sussex. I am honoured to have been chosen as the illustrator for Isabella Tree's book, *Wilding*. Working on this project allowed me to visit the estate many times and see it changing through the seasons. I have to say it was the encounter with red deer that most stays in my memory. Seeing these red deer during the autumn months was truly spectacular and led to the cover image of this book. I was also inspired by watching jays gathering acorns, owls hooting and the joy of hearing nightingales. These encounters with nature are very personal; it is these experiences that I always wanted to express as an artist, and my prints are an attempt to do this.

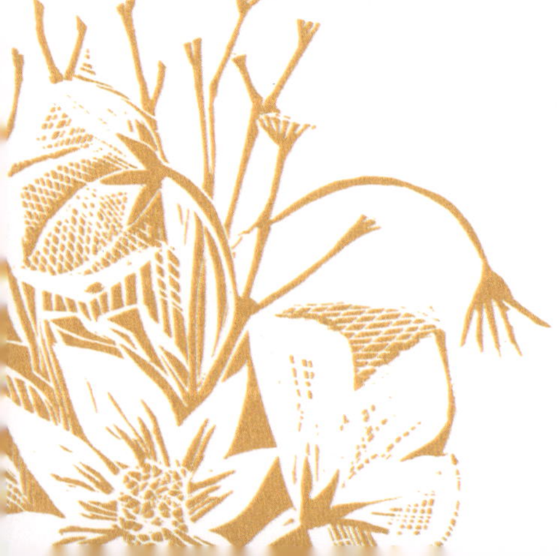

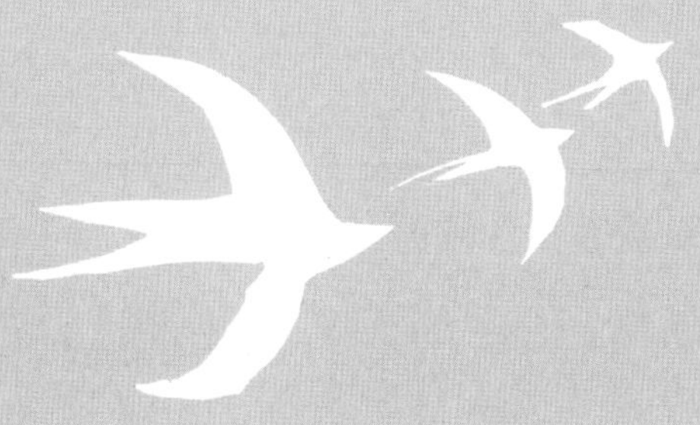

Falling into Autumn is the third in a series of four books that reflect on the seasons. This quartet has its origins in my first book, *A Year Unfolding*, which is a printmaker's view of the changing seasons. In this book about autumn, I have added new images and text to my original thoughts about this season. This book is a new format; a small book that you can put in your pocket to muse on travels and in quiet moments, or a gift book to cherish with others who share my love of nature. The other books in this series are *Spring Unfurled*, *Summer's Hum* and *Winter's Song*.

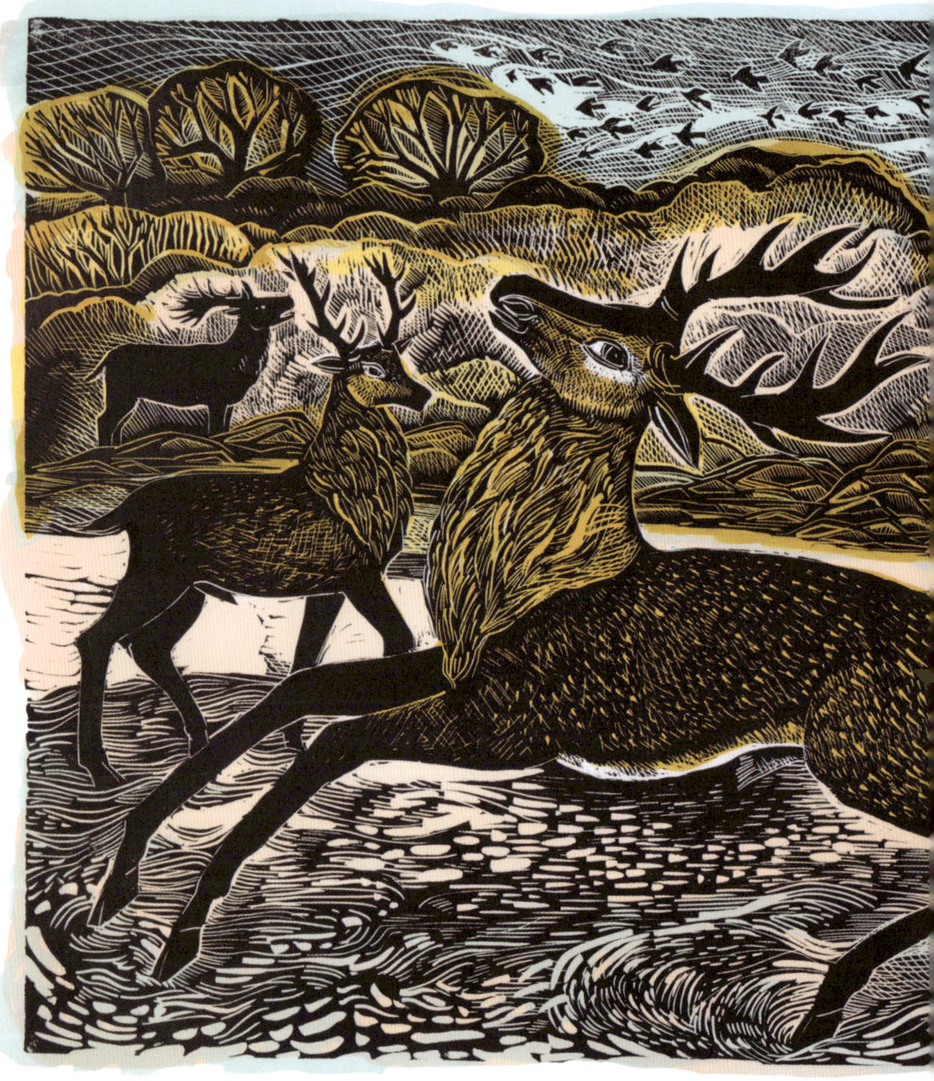

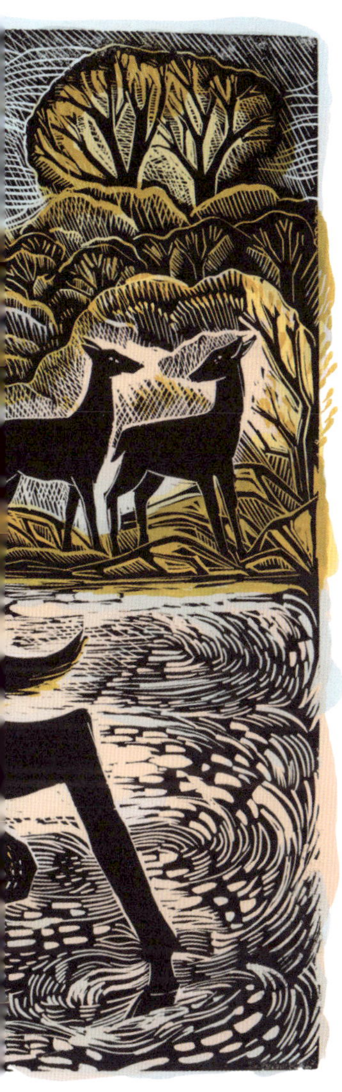

Red deer are big! It is not just their size; they are impressive in their stature. I had still not seen the red deer after my first few days of exploring Knepp. Then one evening, as I was running out of daylight, something was moving through the trees, dry twigs cracking under hooves. I retreated inside the bothy, as I thought it might be approaching deer. And it was! A small herd of red deer came round the edge of the pond, then right past my back door, their beautiful heads reaching up to eat the lower leaves of the trees. I watched, amazed by their size, and by their beauty. I hope I have managed to capture some of the awe I felt on that day in this linocut.

Opposite:
The Common
(Linocut and silkscreen)

There are some gardens that live long in my memory. One such is the garden at Gainsborough's House in Sudbury, Suffolk. This was the birthplace of Thomas Gainsborough and it's now a museum that's open to the public. The garden is dominated by a huge mulberry tree that dates to when Gainsborough was living there. Also, there is an open-access printmaking studio. Over the years, I have done several wood engraving courses there. Making prints in such a historic environment is wonderful. We were able to use the studio well into the evening. Taking breaks in the garden was very special. It felt rather like the setting for the Andrew Marvell poem, 'The Garden', the evening light falling on the mulberry tree, as well as pears, apples and quince.

Opposite:
Pigeons and Pears
(Linocut and silkscreen)

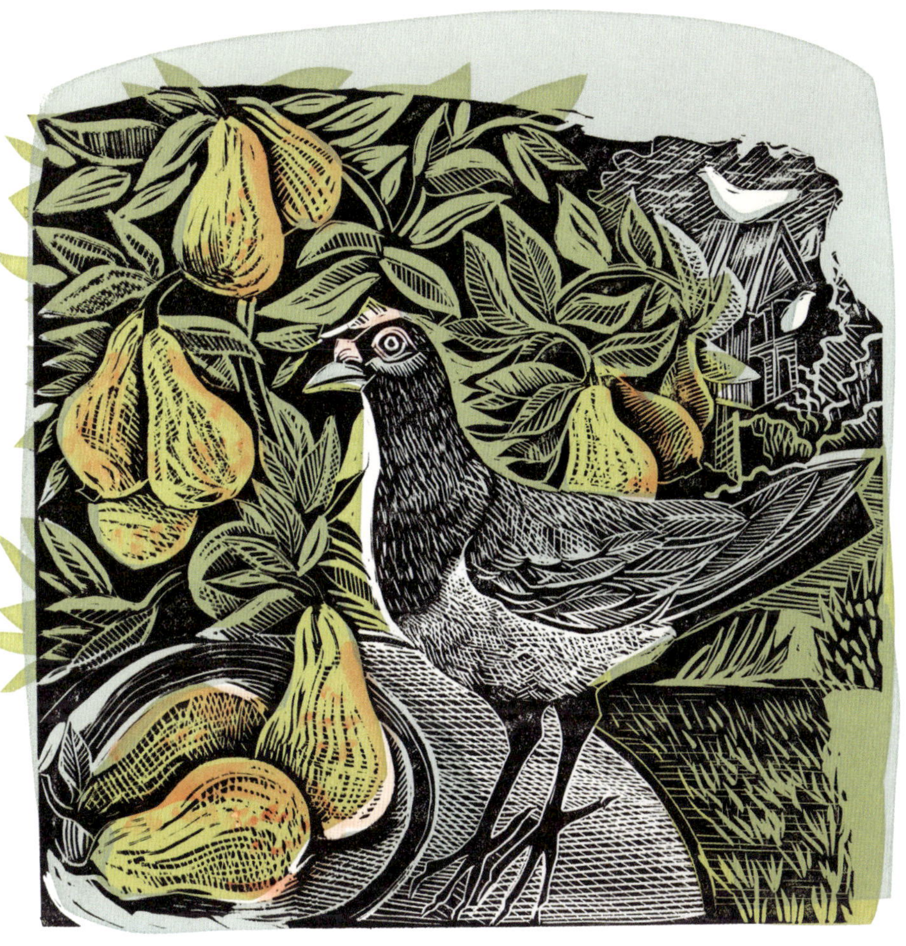

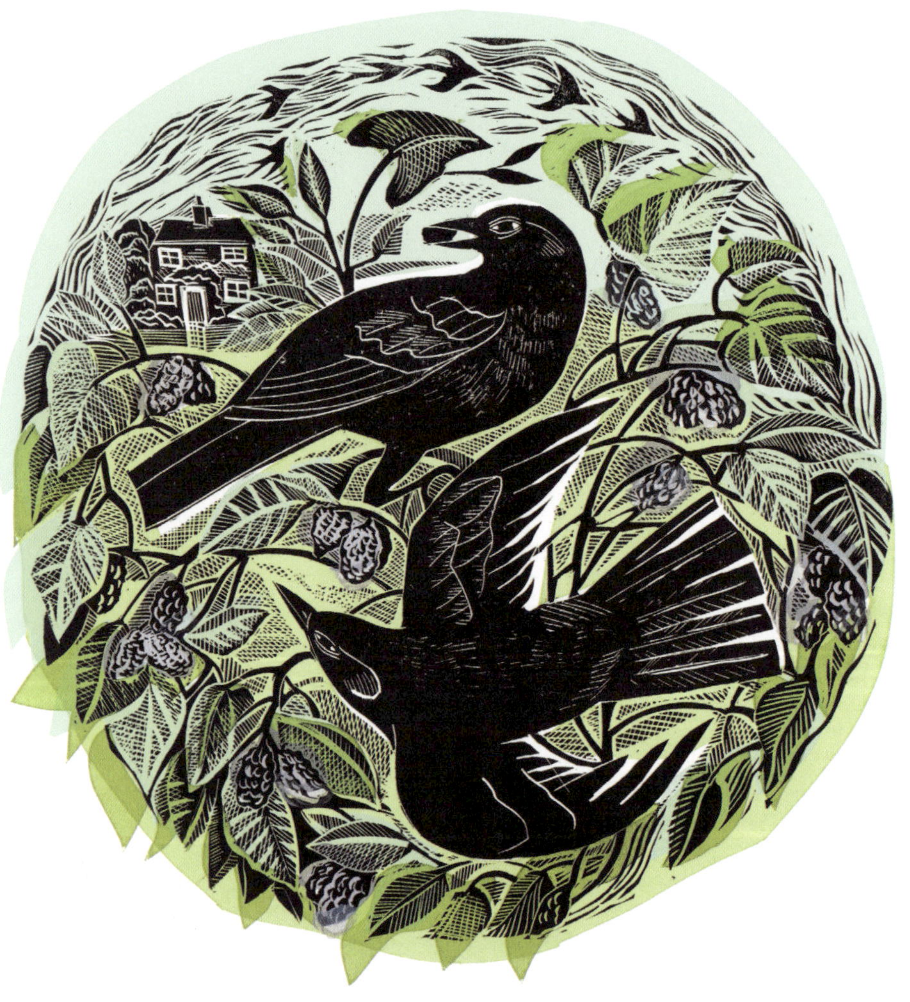

As the autumn season progresses, the reds, oranges and browns of the late summer garden are reflected in the colours of the trees as their leaves begin to turn. By the end of August, the mulberry tree is thick with mulberries. Mark and I first met in a garden with the most magnificent mulberry tree. They are very slow growing and can live to a great age, so we promised ourselves one for our own garden. The fruit has the most remarkable flavour and the one in our garden fruits really well – the lovely black berries are delicious. You have to battle the blackbirds for them; they seem to know as soon as they are ripe and are able to eat a tremendous number every day.

Opposite:
Blackbirds and Mulberry Tree
(Linocut and silkscreen)

As summer draws to a close, the swallows and house martins outside the studio practise their flying skills in preparation for their long journey to Africa. Last year, there were a large number of young birds. They looked like a complex musical score – dots of swallows and house martins swaying on the telephone wire. But then, in a whirl of wings and a mad chattering panic, they all took to the sky. It soon became apparent why they were behaving in this way – there was a hobby! It swooped through the swallow mob, and the adult swallows showed their protective nature towards their young as they dive-bombed the hunter. Fortunately, no swallows were caught by the hobby on this occasion.

Opposite:
Heading Home
(Linocut and silkscreen)

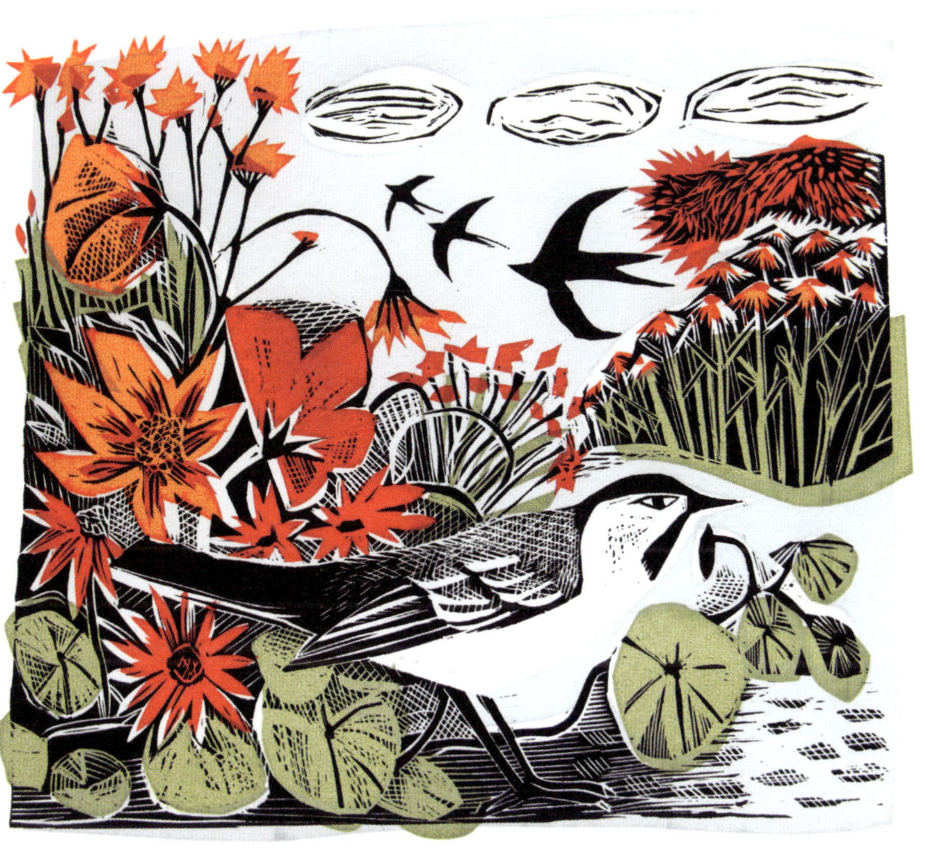

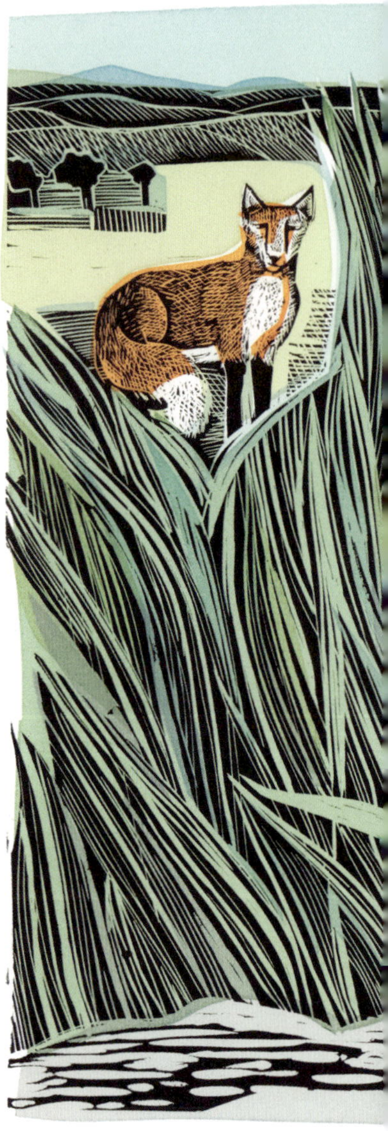

During the 1980s, my sister, Sarah Harding, and I were both art students. During the holidays, we retreated to my father's house on the Welsh borders. He was not living there at the time, so the cottage became a refuge for art students and other creatures. Eventually, Sarah lived full-time in the cottage, gathering a troop of pets around her. The troop included one horse, one lamb (later rehomed to a flock), four dogs, three cats, a Chinese quail that ran around the sitting room and a small flock of chickens. The chickens were a mixture of breeds that clucked and roamed around the garden, but they knew not to stray too far from home. There was always the threat of foxes, often seen in the fields around the cottage, their coats gleaming gold in late-autumn sunlight as they dashed across the countryside.

Opposite:
Autumn Chickens
(Linocut and silkscreen)

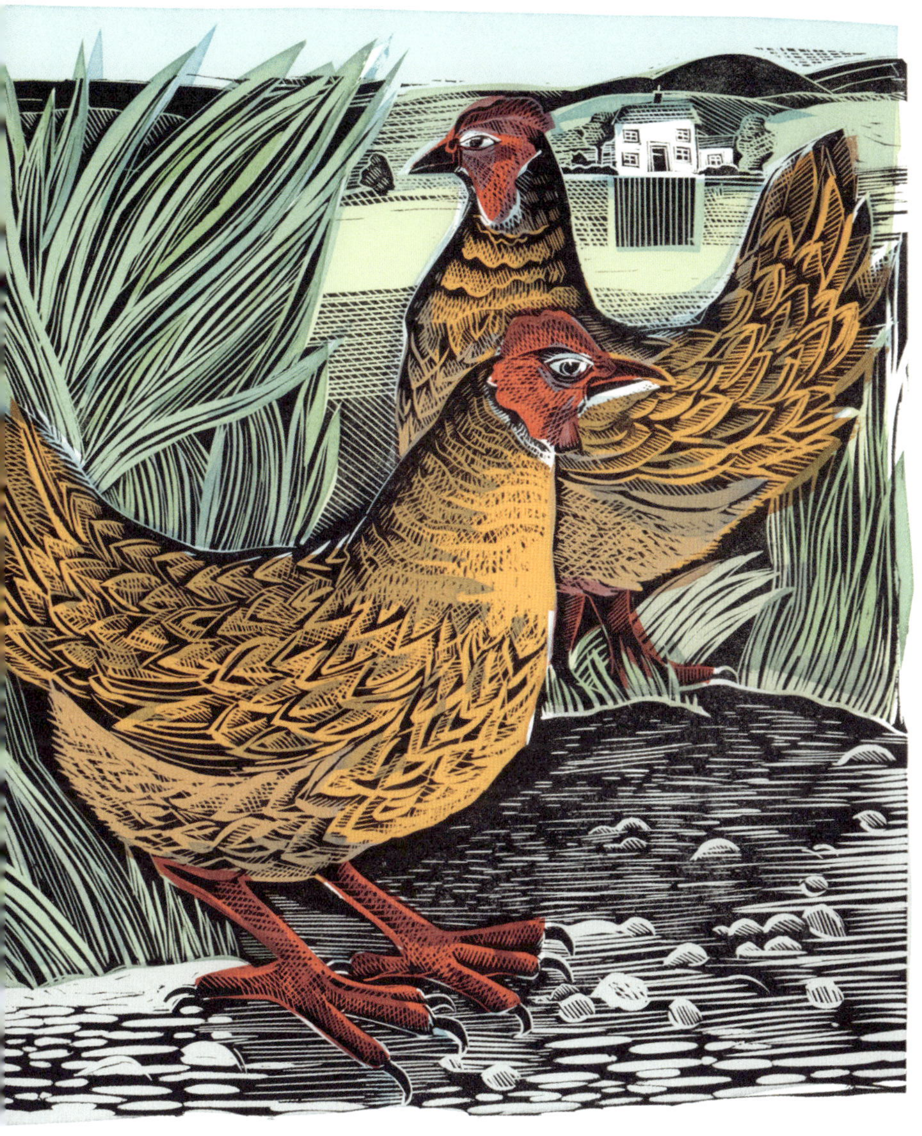

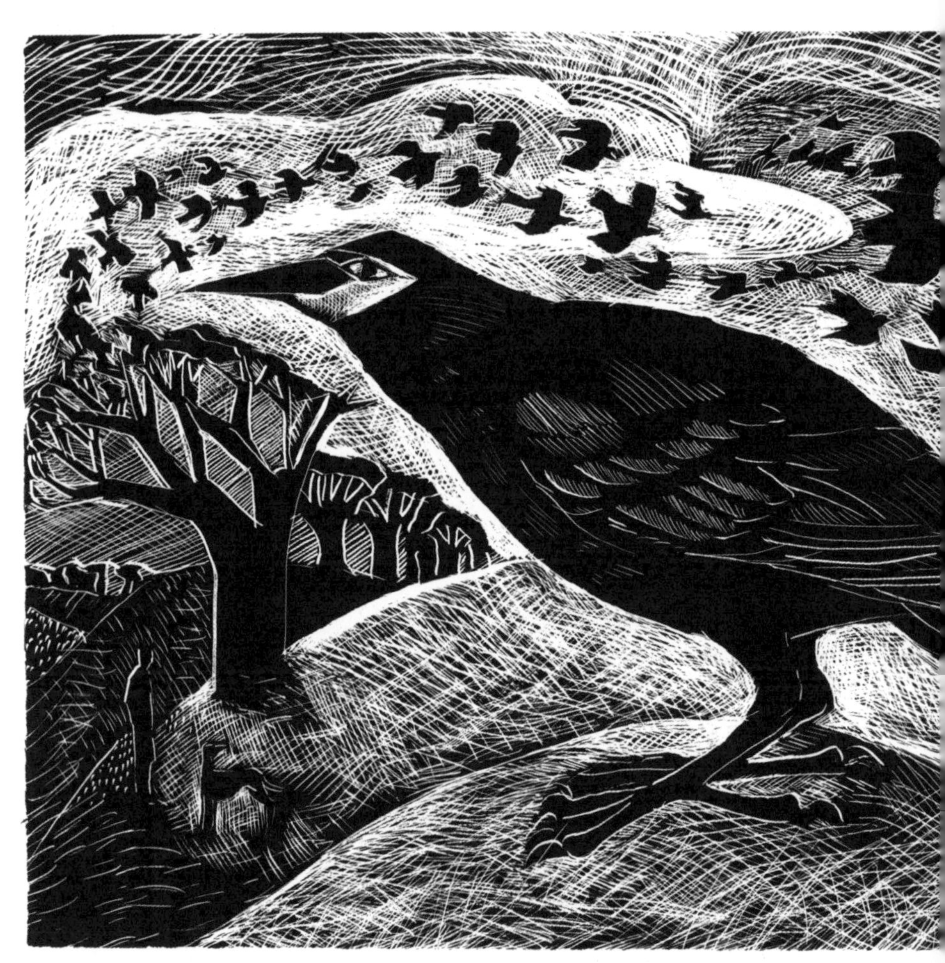

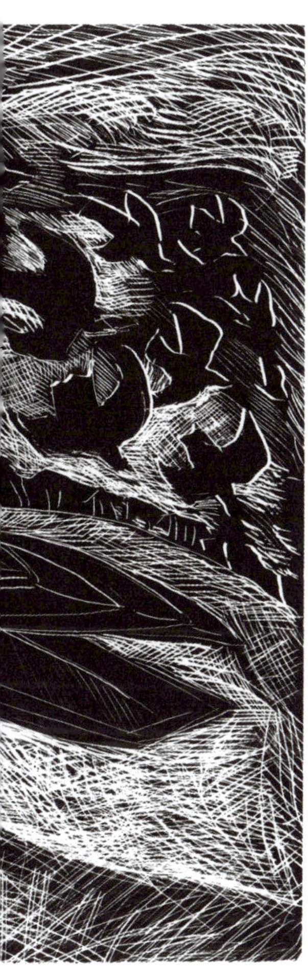

Opposite:
Rooks and More Rooks
(Scraper board)

Rooks are often disliked, but I find them the most magical of birds. Rooks have, for many generations, been shot at as they are seen as vermin, but they are misunderstood. Rooks are both very intelligent and very social; in the winter months, they gather with other corvids, such as jackdaws, forming impressive noisy flocks. We are lucky to have one of these colonies on the edge of the village. If you get to this site at just the right time, you can see hundreds of these black birds returning home to their treetops after a day foraging for food. Seeing this massive flock as the light is getting low is truly spectacular, not only for the beauty of such a sight but also for the sheer volume of noise.

Sleep No More was an illustration commissioned by Faber & Faber for a P. D. James book of the same title. The image is of a friend's house that I was staying at in the Cotswolds. The house was a grand place but rather faded from its days of glory. All the windows needed replacing and the roof leaked. It felt just a bit ominous and therefore was the perfect setting for a murder mystery.

Opposite:
Sleep No More
(Linocut and silkscreen)

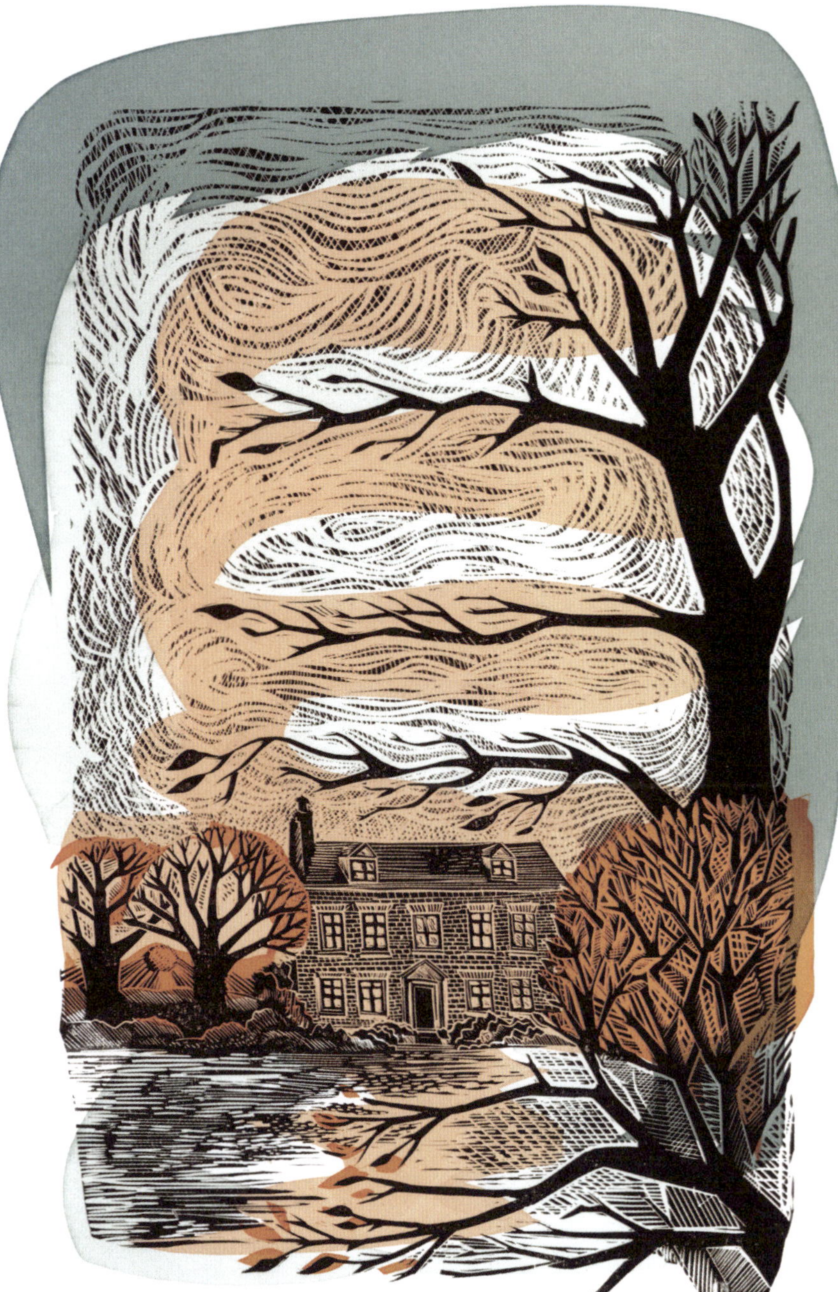

Whippets have been part of our family for many years. Our first sighthound, Syd, was a rescue lurcher who came with separation anxiety – the solution we found was to get another dog. So, Tiffany whippet arrived and for many years we had whippets by the pair. Today we just have Oaty, who is happy as a single dog but very much makes our home a whippet's place.

Opposite:
A Whippet Place
(Linocut and silkscreen)

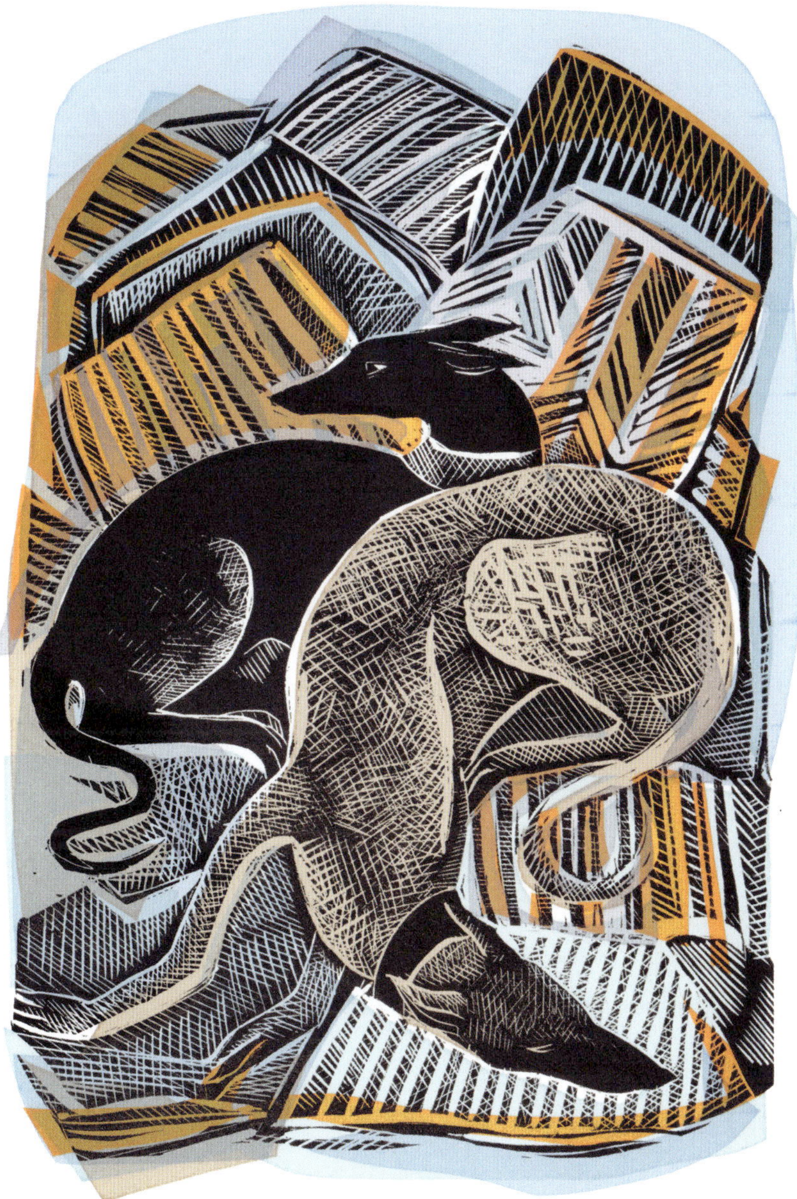

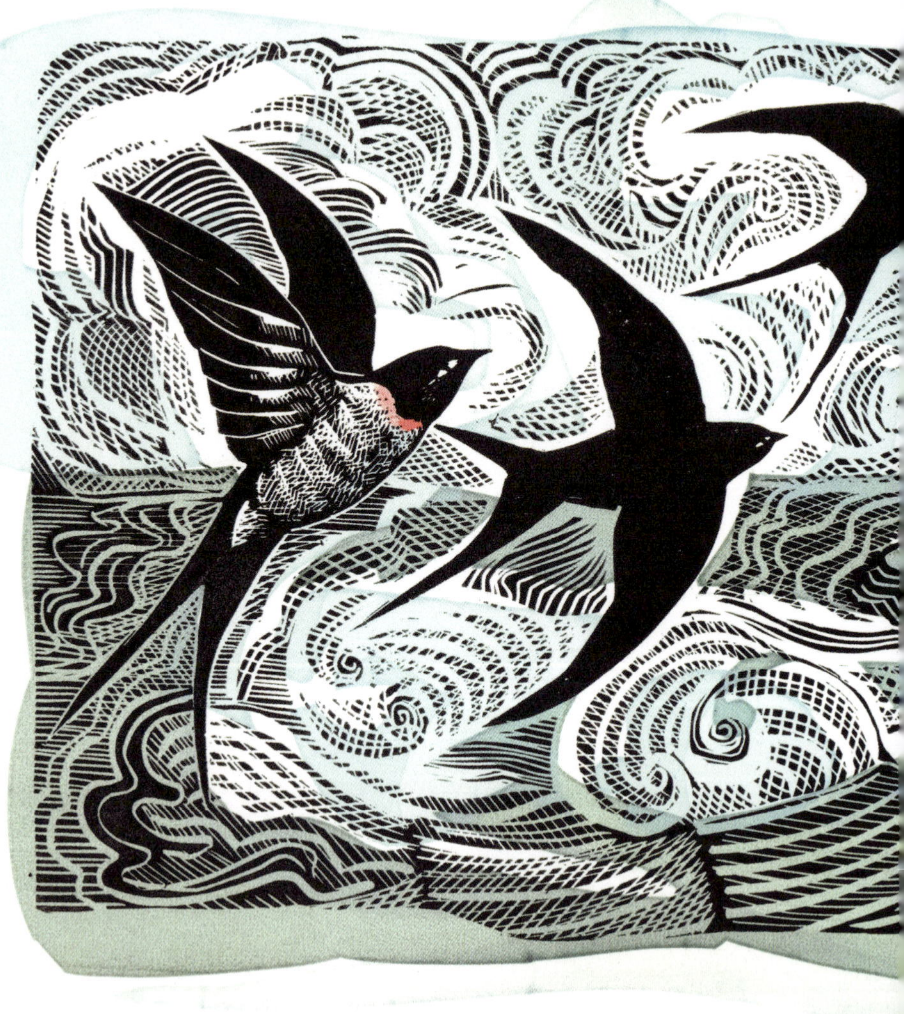

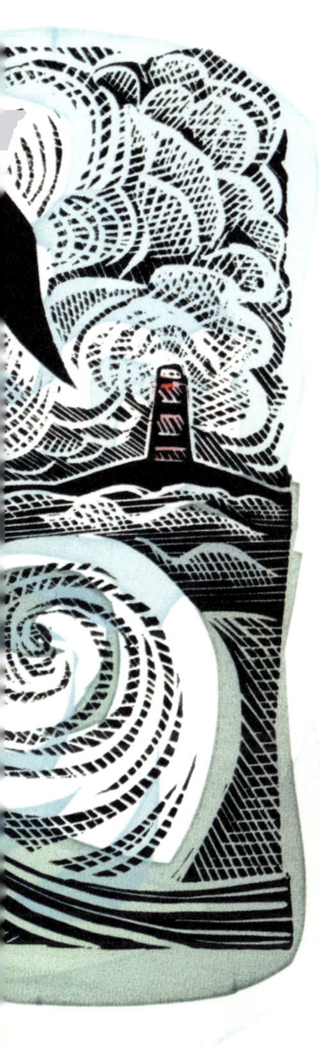

Goodbyes – the gathering clouds of swallows, geese in storms flying over the boat, the ghost of a barn owl over the water at Snape . . .

When sailing is done, it seems to coincide with the time when we say goodbye to the swallows, house martins and swifts.

Opposite:
Swallows and Seas
(Linocut and silkscreen)

Autumn in Suffolk or Norfolk is when geese gather in great flocks. The flocks are a mixture of pink-footed, Canada and greylag geese. These great squadrons of geese fly in formation over our boat, *Windsong*, at what seems to be at the same time every evening with a volume of noise that it is hard to believe. They follow the course of the river, looming out of the dusk, then part in formation round the mast of the boat before rejoining in the sound bouncing off the water. Contrast the incredible quiet of the day to the echoes honking off the still water – their voices are not tuneful but play their part in the beauty of being on the Butley River.

Opposite:
Canada Geese at the Butley
(Linocut and silkscreen)

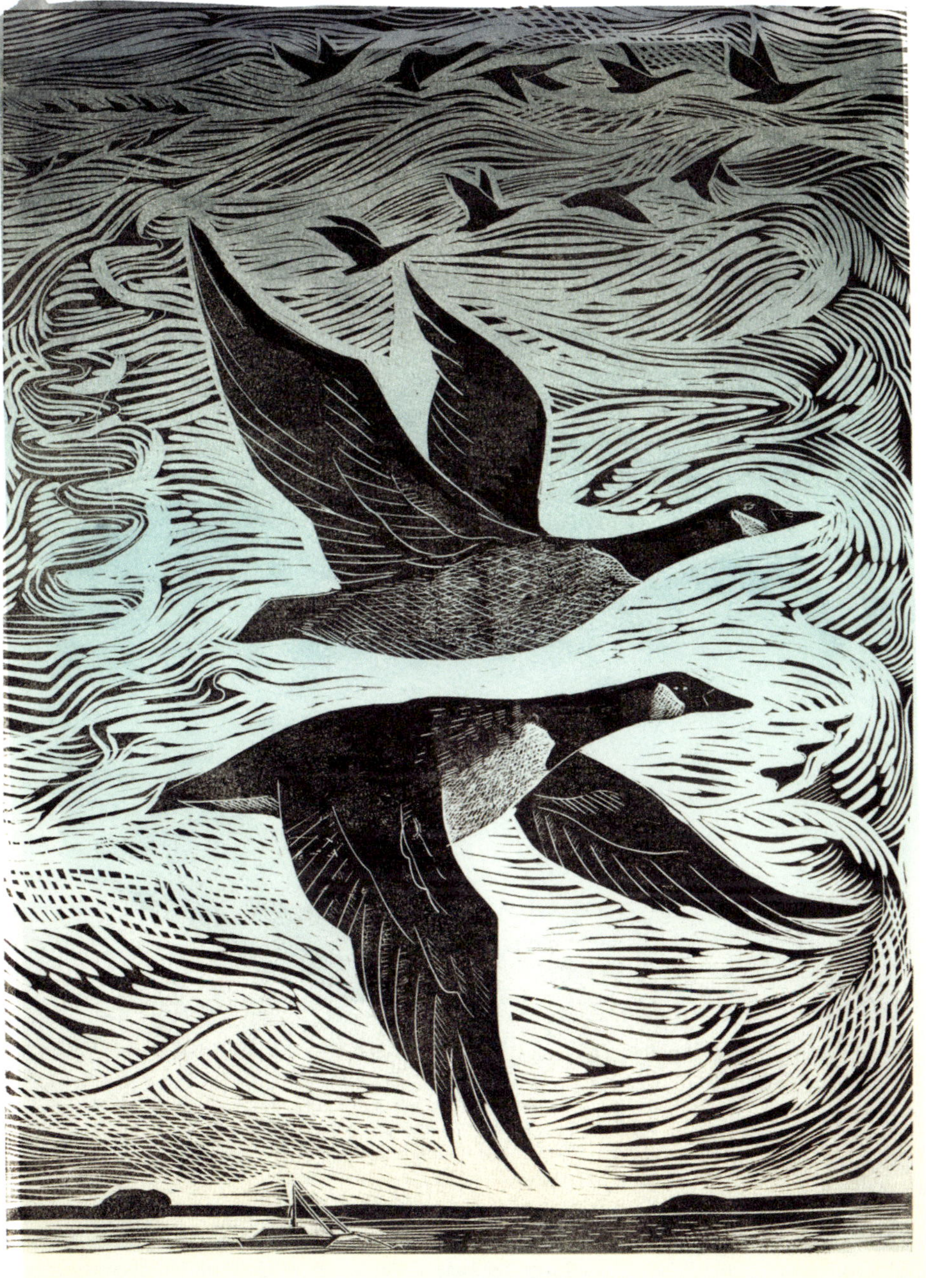

I have always enjoyed travelling on my own. Time alone allows you to think and look in a way that is different to travelling in company. In my twenties, these trips were mainly done by bike and train. The trip from Inverness to Ullapool was very memorable, not only for the spectacular landscape, but because it was the first time I saw wild red deer. The deer seemed to become one with the autumnal landscape they were set against, the colour of the deer and the colour of the bracken blending. It was only when they moved that they became visible.

Opposite:
Deer in Bracken
(Linocut and silkscreen)

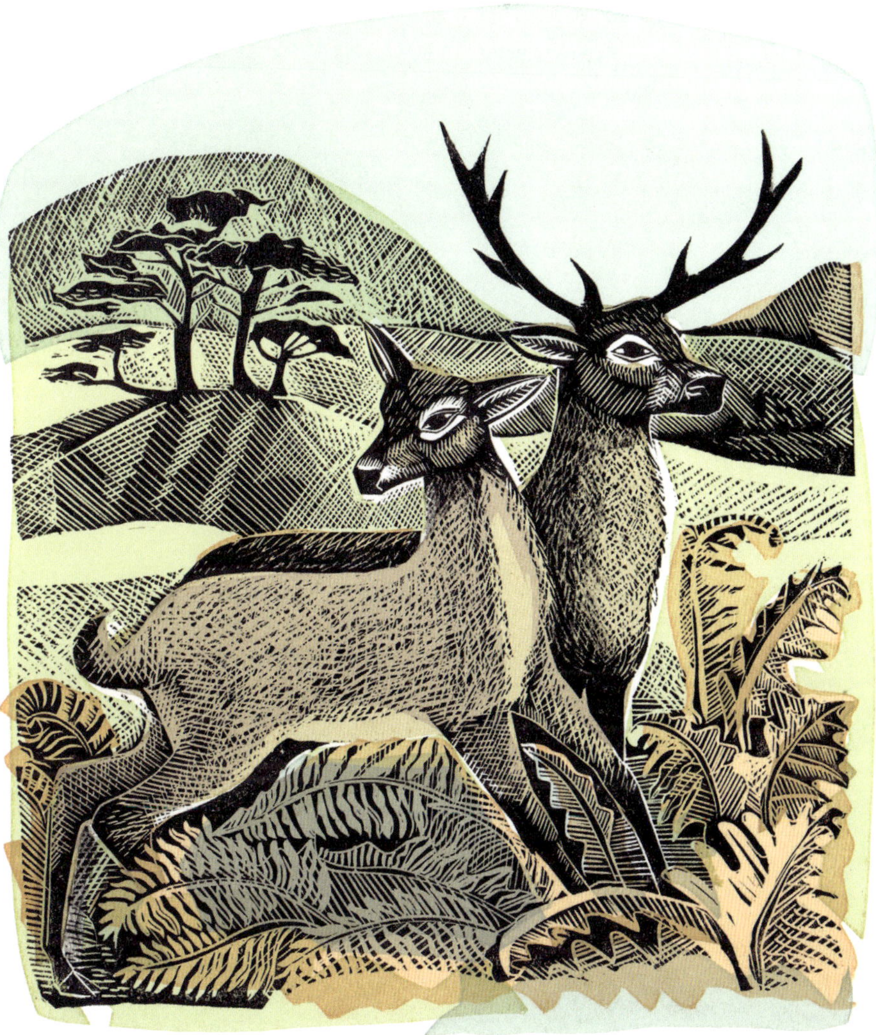

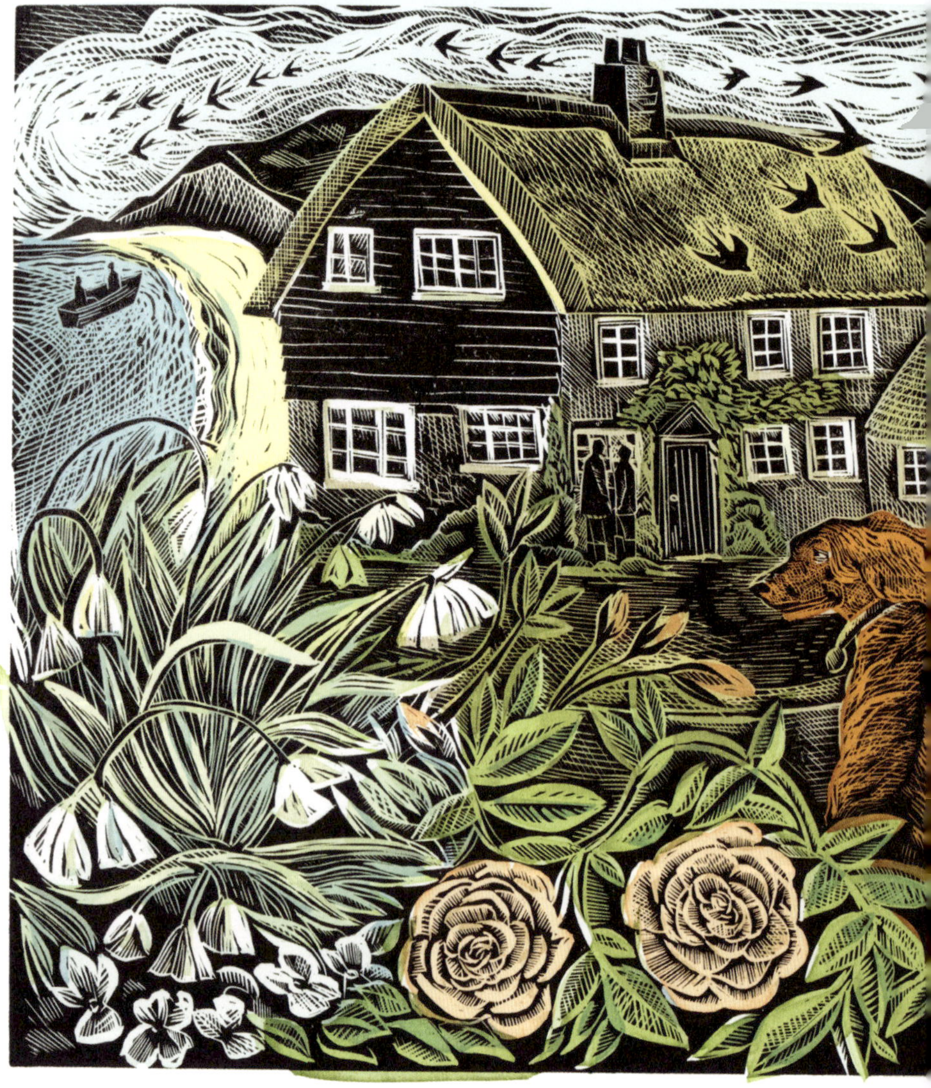

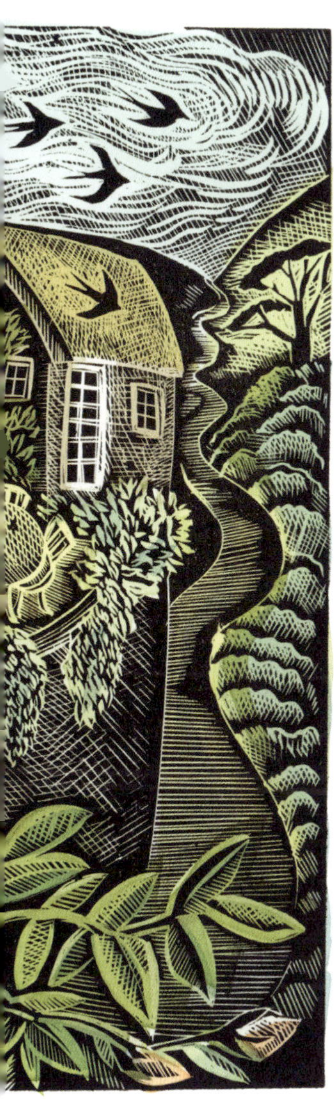

One of the last of the summer trips is to North Devon. I have two friends, Lyndon and Matt, who live in Lee, near Ilfracombe, and visiting them is always a great treat. They live just a stone's throw from Lee Bay in the most idyllic thatched country cottage. The wooded valley shelters wildlife and it contrasts with the ruggedness of the North Devonshire coastline.

Opposite:
Rose Cottage
(Linocut and silkscreen)

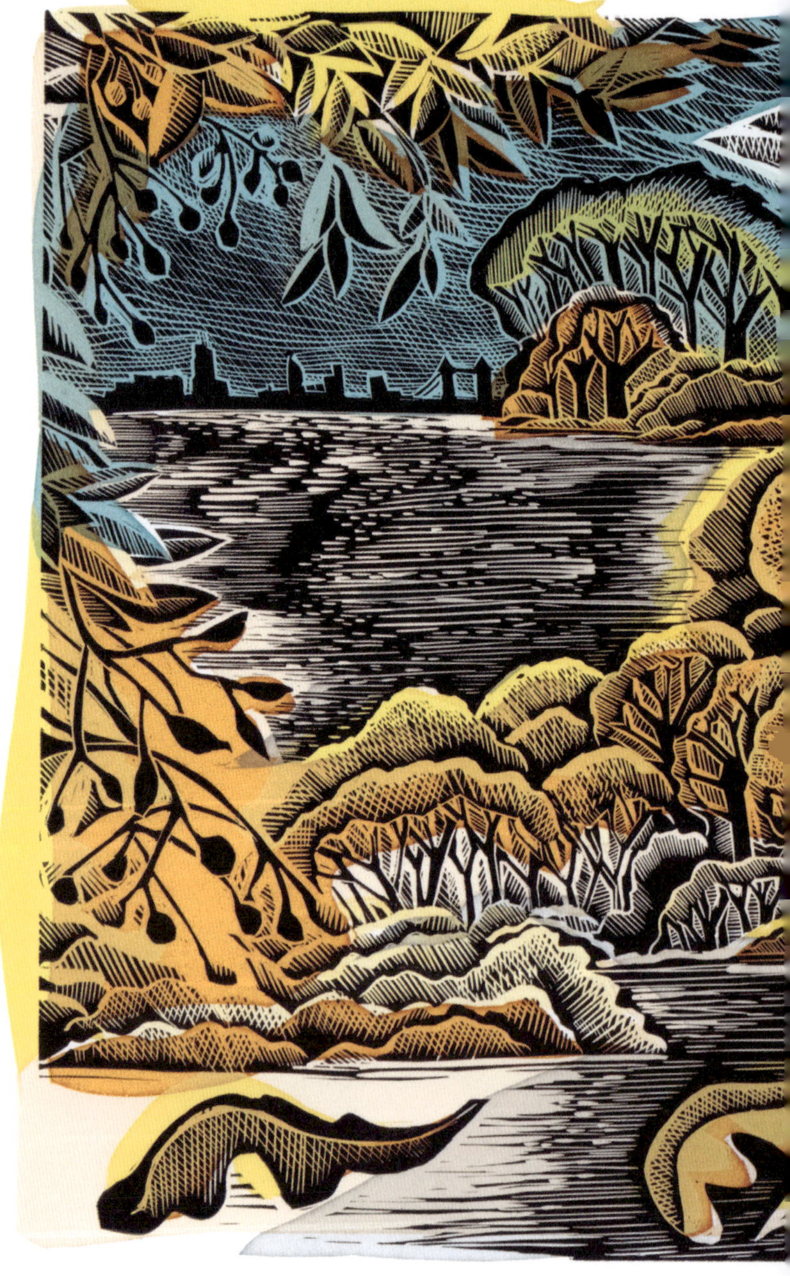

Right:
October Owl
(Linocut and
silkscreen)

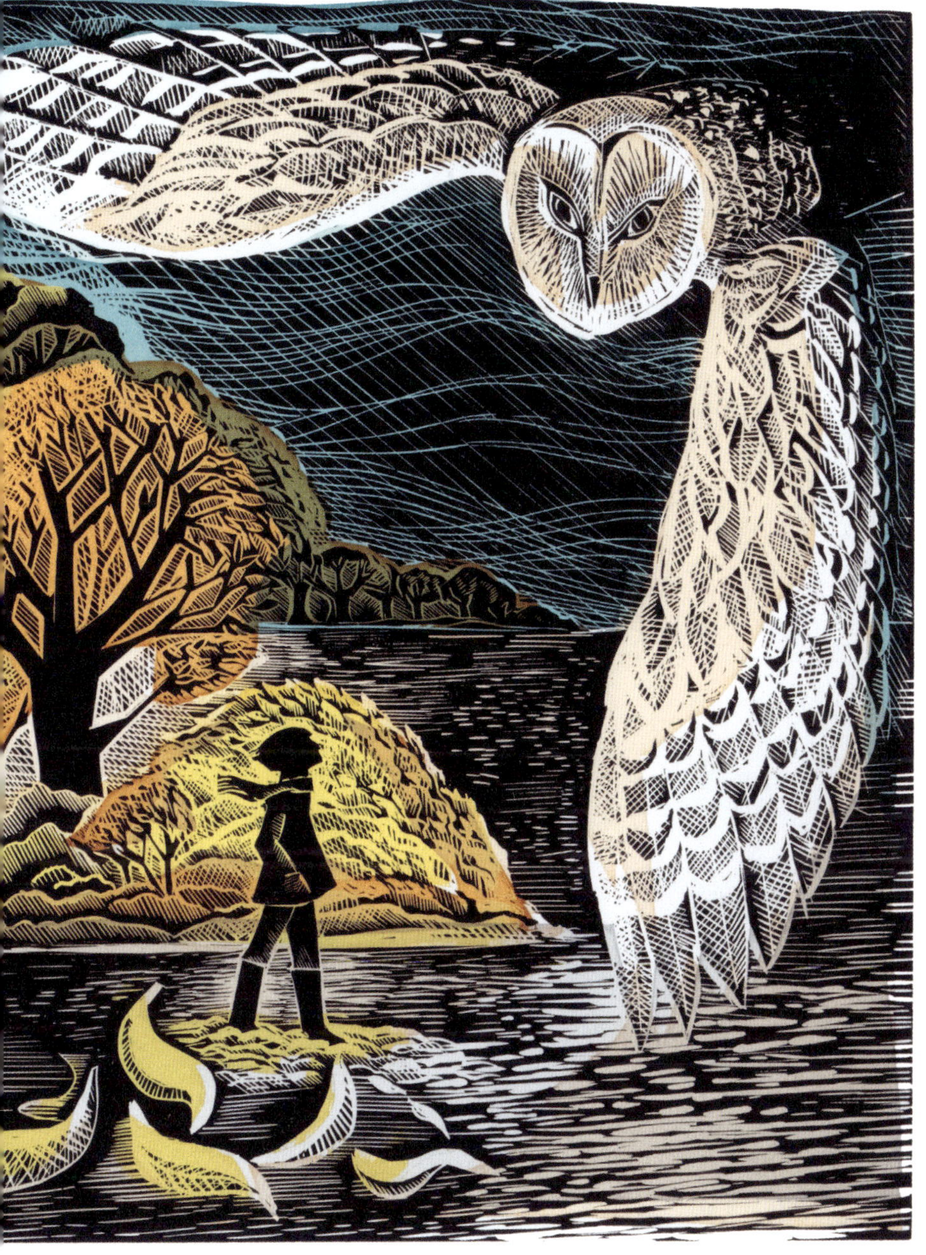

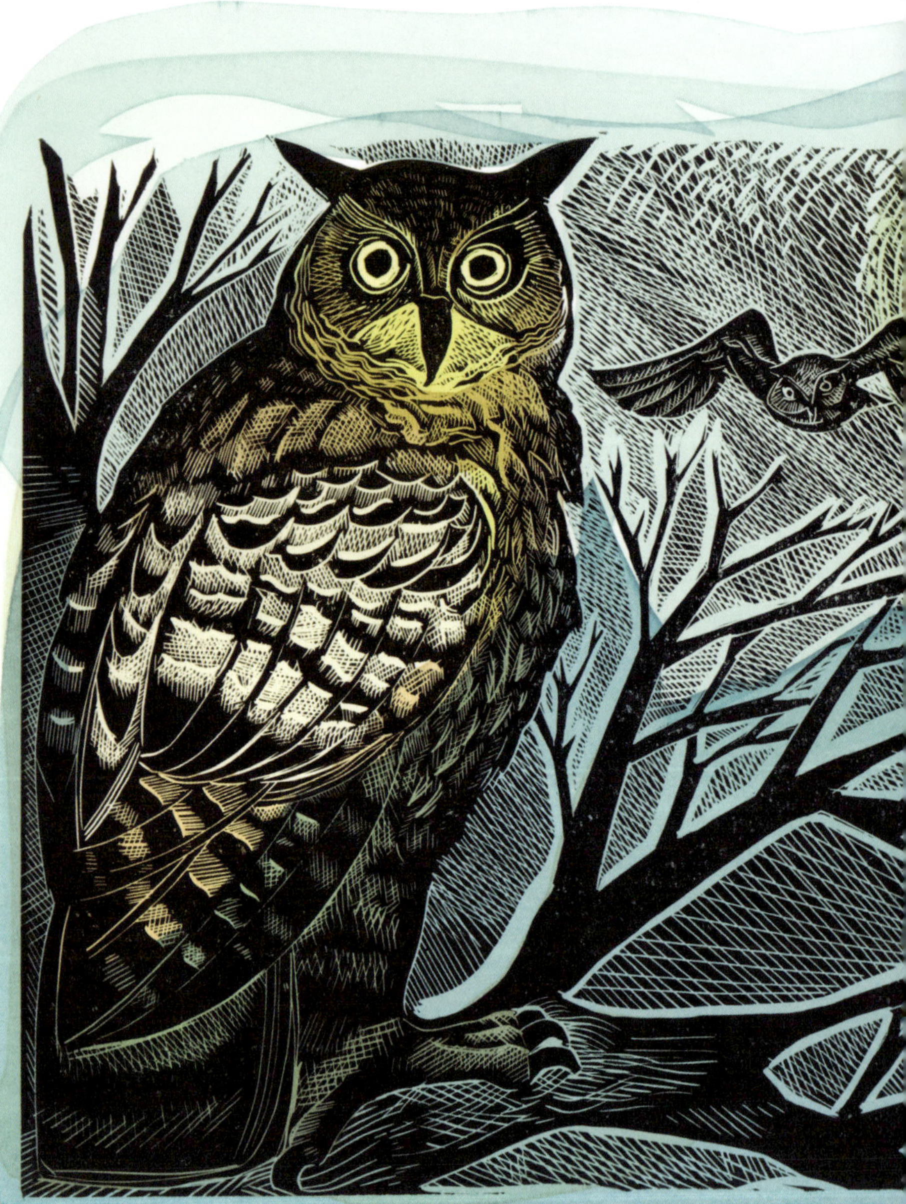

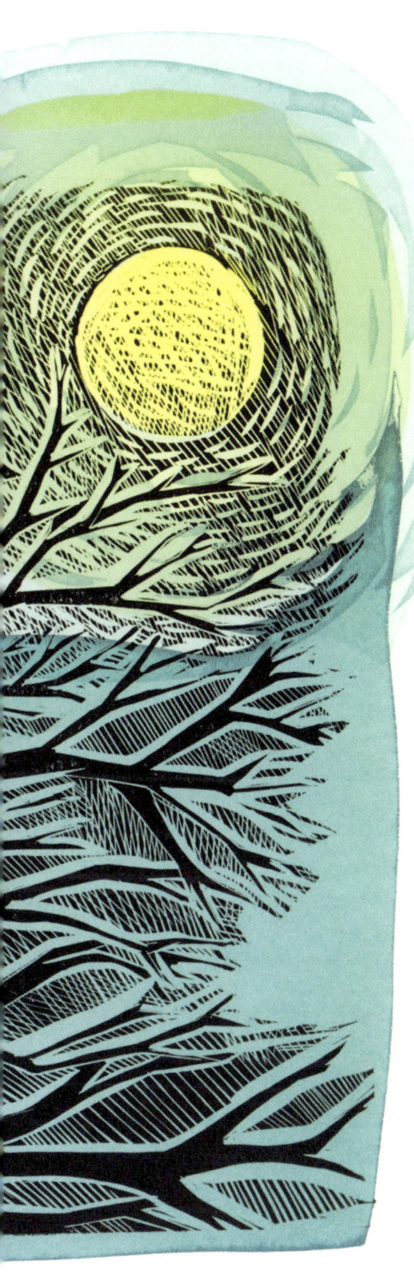

Observing nature and light inspires my printmaking. Perhaps it is on our boat, *Windsong,* that I am most aware of nature and light. We often sleep in our small cabin with the door open. This allows us to see the evening fade to night, the dawn break. If I'm awake, I can hear night-time sounds of herons, owls and nightjars.

Opposite:
Owl and Moon
(Linocut and silkscreen)

For me, gardens have always been about the wildlife they attract, as well as being places of beauty. My friends, Sarah and Jules, who live in our village are of the same mindset. They keep a telescope poised and ready in their conservatory for viewing their resident hedgehogs. Hedgehogs have become much rarer garden visitors than they used to be, so seeing this troop of hogs trundling around their garden is a delight and a very special event.

Opposite:
Hidden Hedgehog
(Linocut and silkscreen)

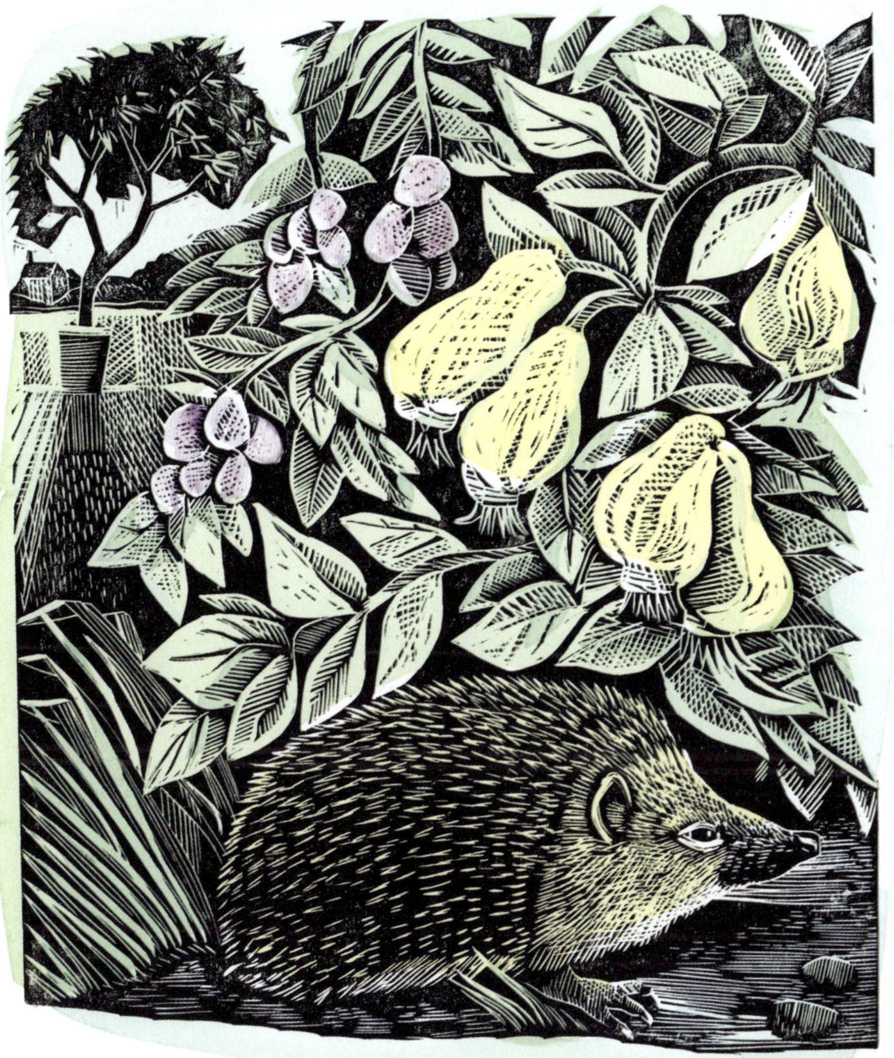

Seeing nature at night-time can be particularly rewarding, perhaps because it feels unusual; it is when the world is quiet, and it is often a solitary experience.

Nature seeks time away from humans and night-time is its best opportunity for this. Nocturnal animals materialise in the time of day that is their hunting ground. Foxes cross city roads, their red coats glowing in street lighting as they forage on what they can find in the detritus left behind by humans. Hooting owls mark out their territory; snuffling badgers emerge from their setts.

Opposite:
Owl, Hill and Fox
(Linocut and silkscreen)

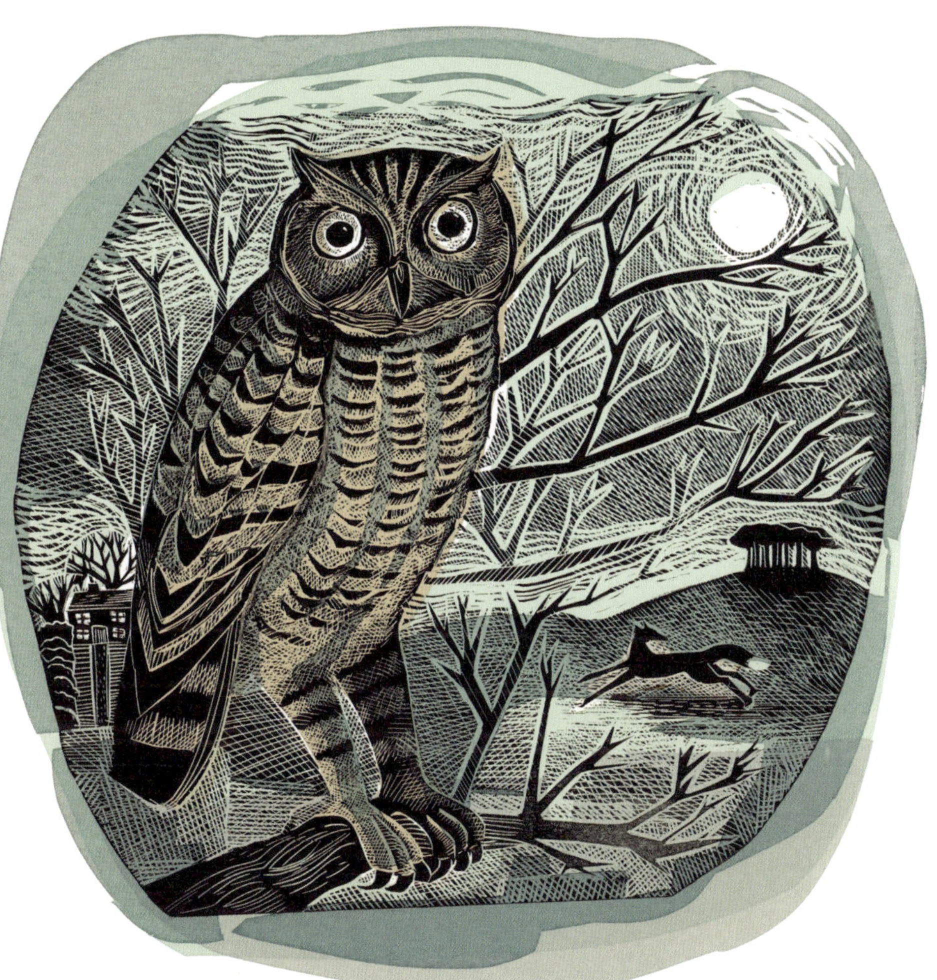

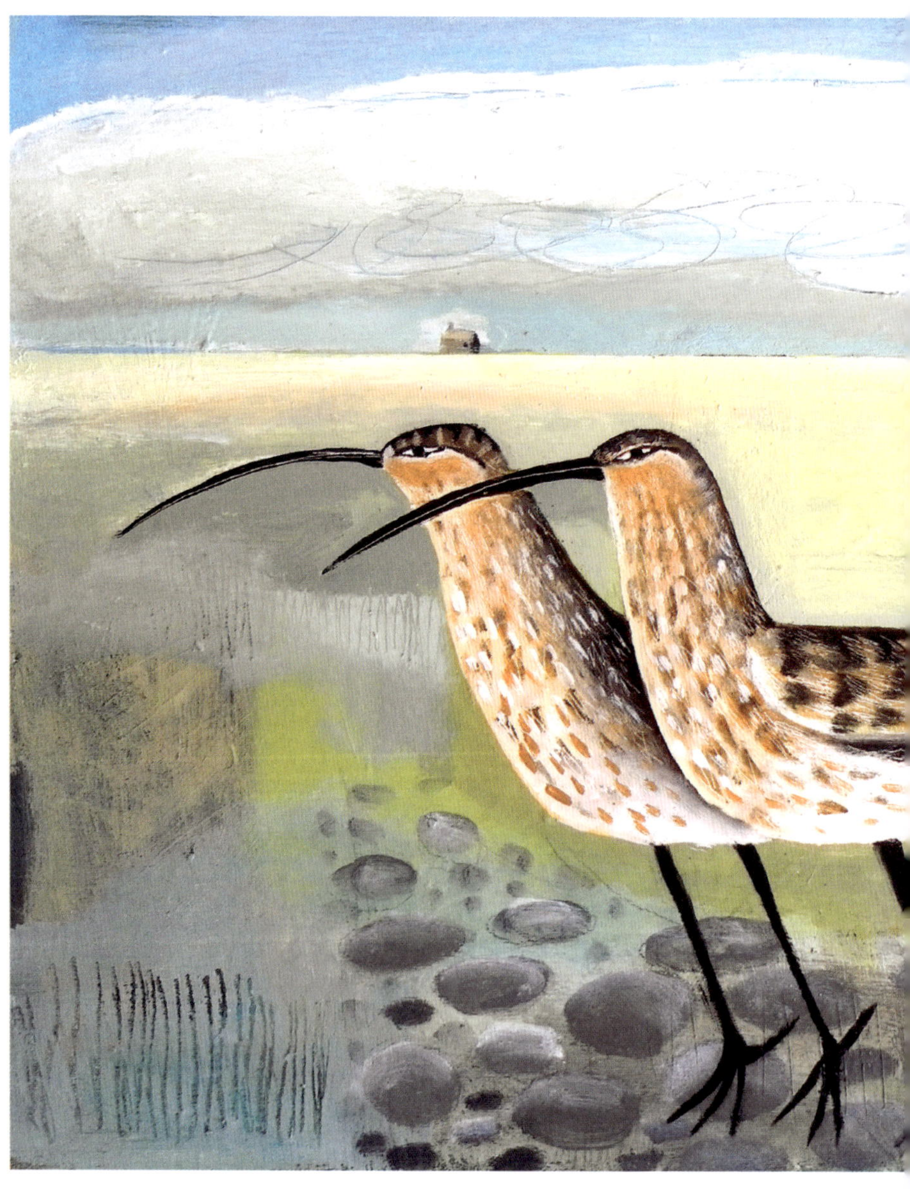

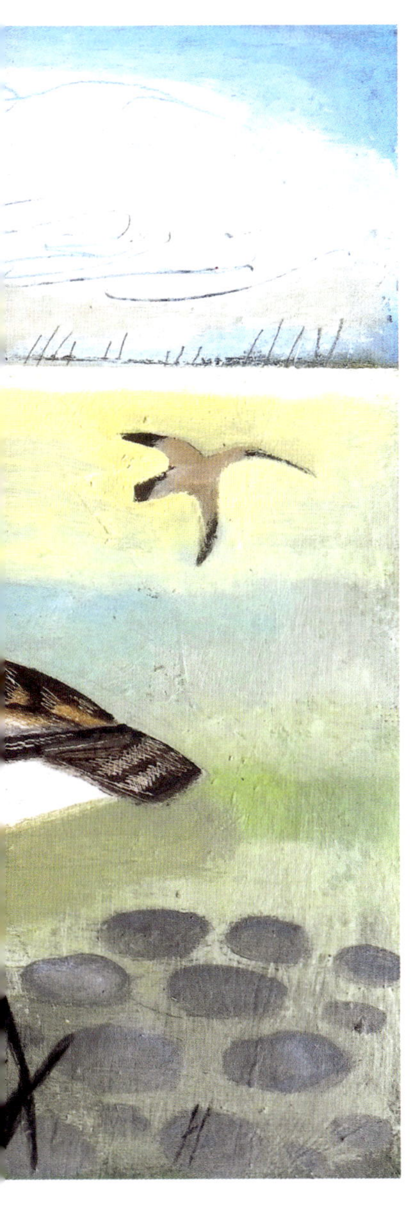

Autumn time on the North Norfolk coast is noisy. Squadrons of migrating geese gather in their tens of thousands, filling the big skies of Norfolk and announcing their presence in loud honking calls. The V formation of the birds follow each other, wave after wave, a pattern of geese that stitch the sky together in a bird blanket of noise. But more than the geese, it is the call of the curlews that inspires me. On autumn evenings, the salt marsh at Morston echoes with the haunting whistle of curlews. They rise in a sudden swoop; their bent bills vibrating with their beautiful song. I am always dumbstruck by this sound, which leaves me rooted to the spot and unable to describe the feeling of being in the presence of curlews calling.

Opposite:
Two Curlews at Morston
(Painting)

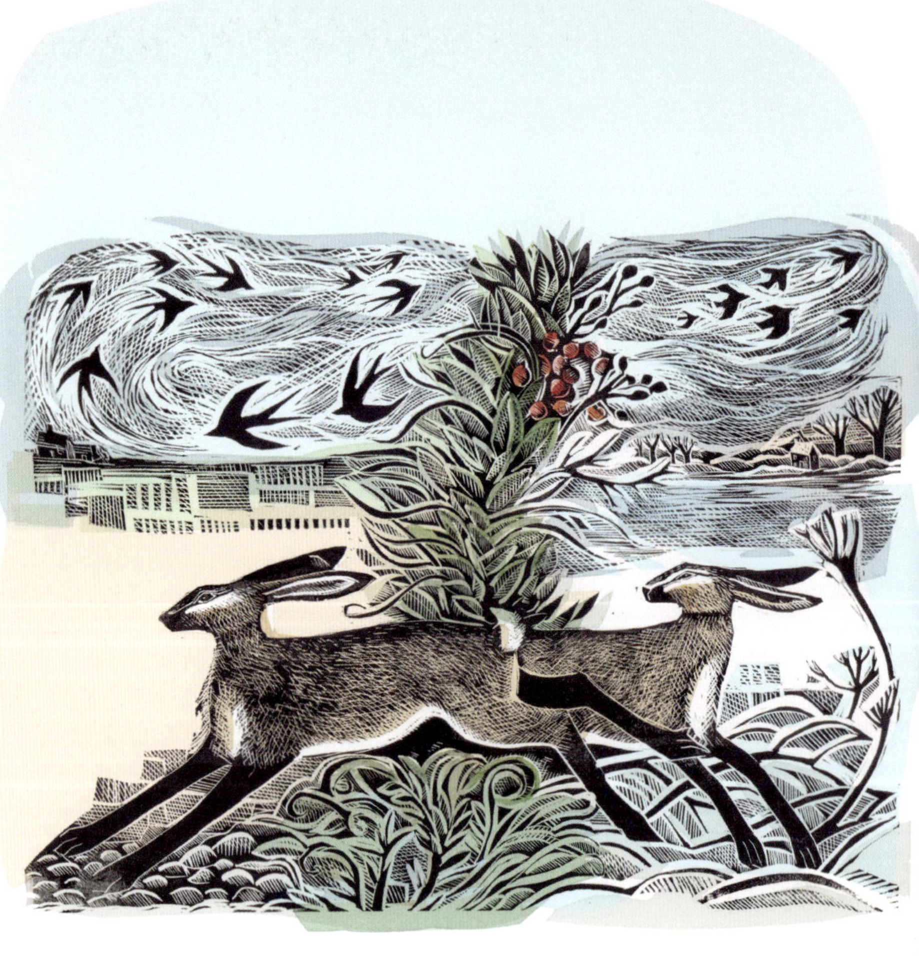

Fields, skies, sea waves and still water are the backdrops I use in my prints; birds and other wildlife the characters I place upon them to make my artwork. Much of the inspiration for my artwork comes from watching the year unfold from winter to spring to summer and autumn while I work at my desk.

Opposite:
A Year Unfolding
(Linocut and silkscreen)

One of the best aspects of midday sun in our garden in Wing is having lunch outside. We have a permanent table set up outside the studio that is now very weather-beaten. Mark and I both love eating outside, so at any opportunity the bottom of the garden becomes our dining room. As the view is over farmland, we are quite often treated to the sight of a scuttling partridge or a beautiful pair of bullfinches.

Opposite:
Bullfinch and Pear Tree
(Linocut and silkscreen)

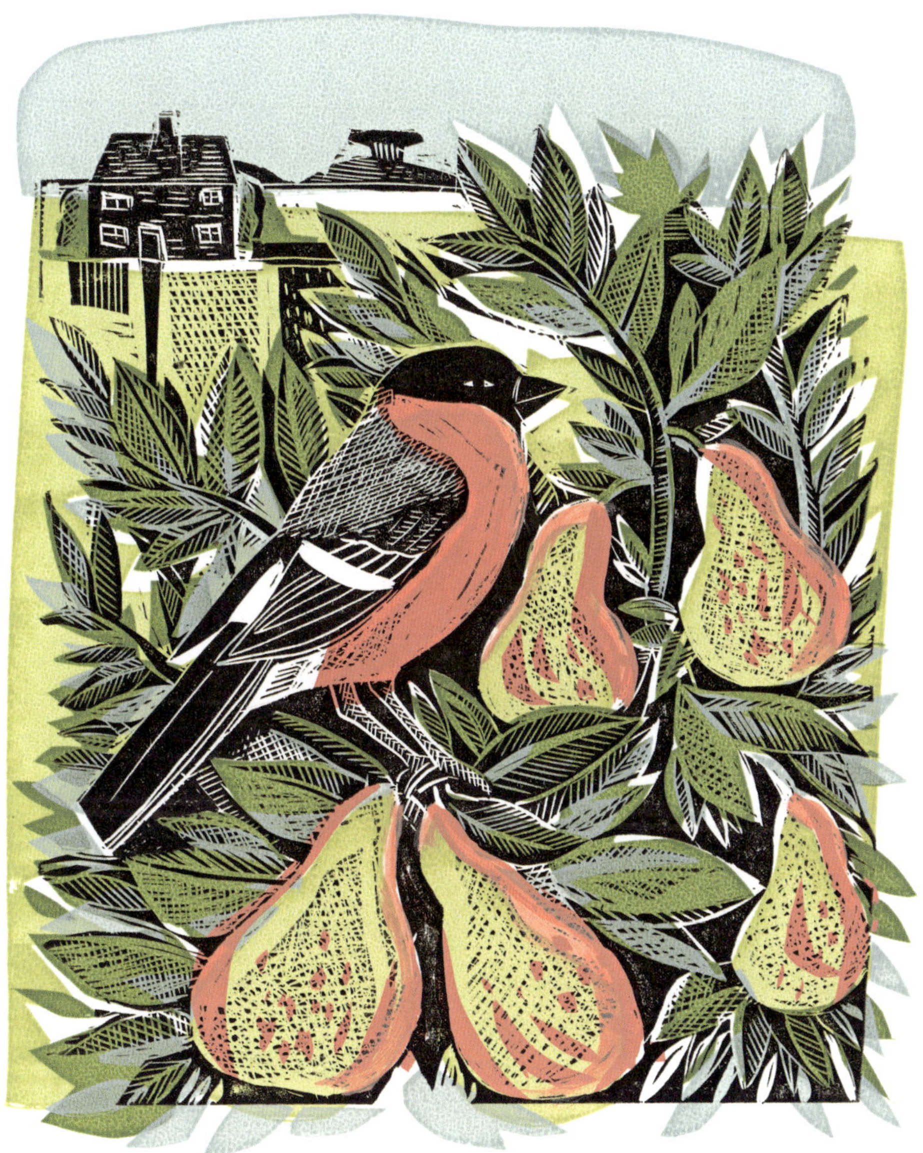

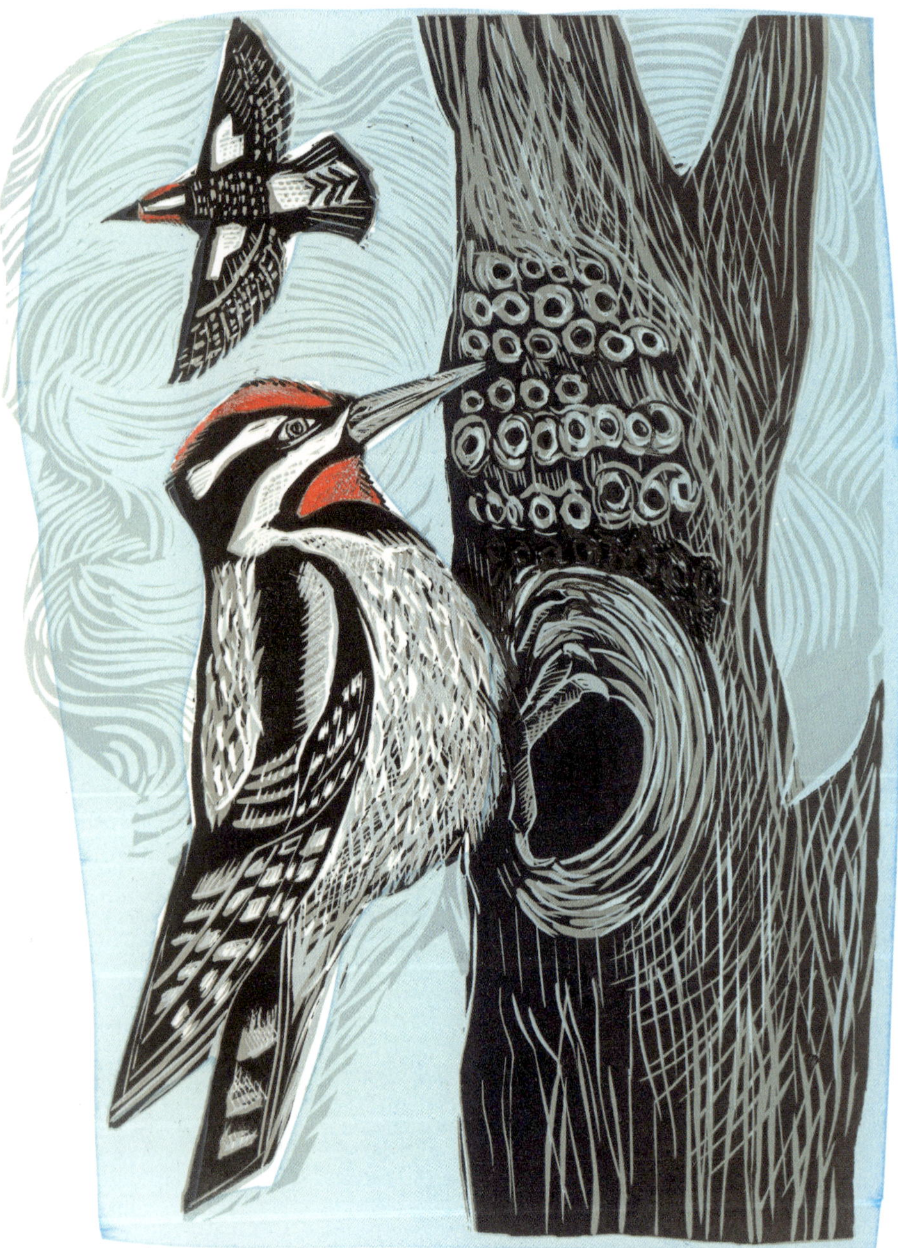

Opposite:
Great Spotted Woodpecker
(Linocut and silkscreen)

We are lucky to see woodpeckers regularly in our village. The Green Woodpeckers are the most common, but definitely the most distinctive are the Lesser and Great Woodpeckers. They are instantly recognisable by their black and white plumage topped with a red crest. In springtime, you can hear them drumming on the oak tree, but by autumn the drumming has stopped.

Blackbirds are great garden companions: they hop through the borders and in summer sing from the walnut tree. In the autumn, they rummage through fallen leaves looking for food, shuffling through the debris with their feet and beaks. They are also inspiring to draw, paint and print. I like their solid black and brown form that contrasts with the foliage of the garden.

Opposite:
Blackbird
(Linocut and silkscreen)

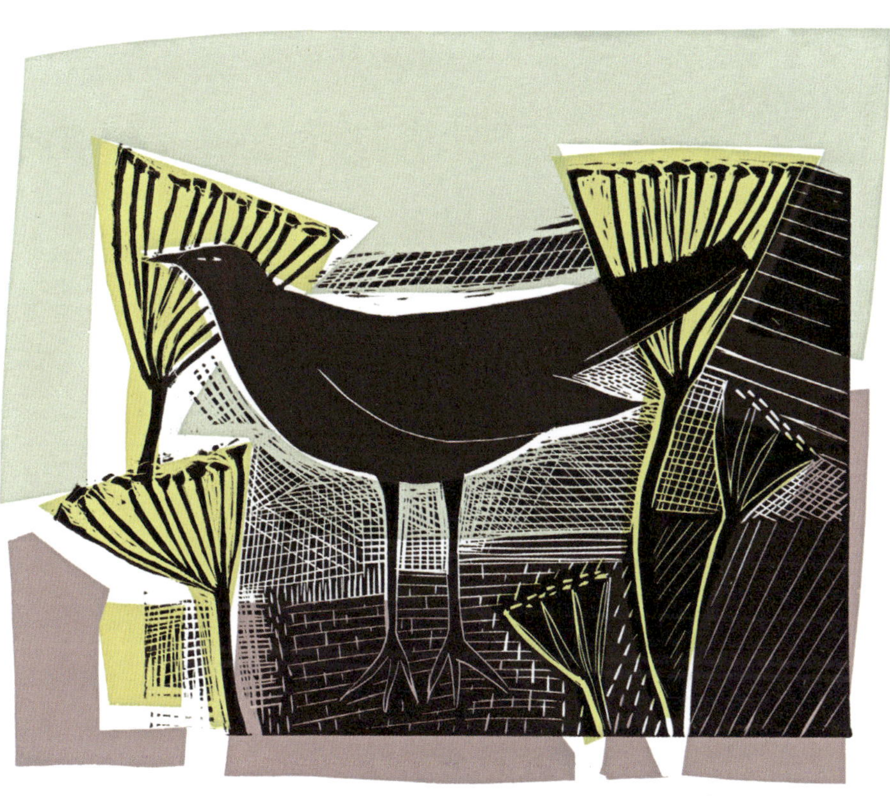

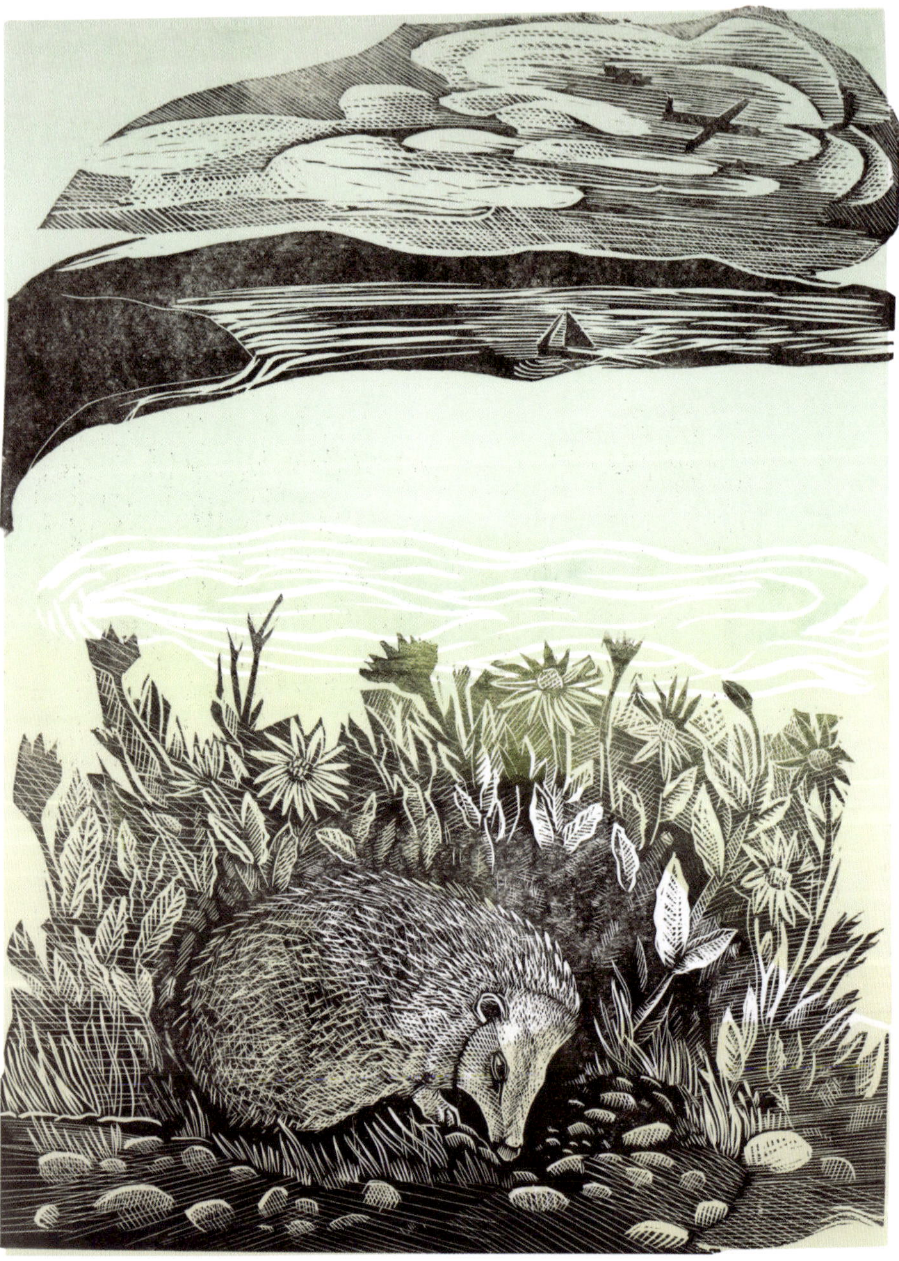

Mark and I visited the Channel Islands on *Windsong* in 2018. Sadly, Alderney was the one island we didn't manage to get to, so we will have to go back. The print *Hedgehog at Alderney* was one of several illustrations commissioned for *Country Living* magazine to accompany a series of articles about the islands. Alderney hedgehogs are particularly interesting as, unlike the rest of the UK's hedgehog population, they're thriving. This is due to the fact there are no predators and a large percentage of them are blond. It is therefore thought that they are easier to see in evening light by drivers, who can safely steer clear of them.

Opposite:
Hedgehog at Alderney
(Linocut)

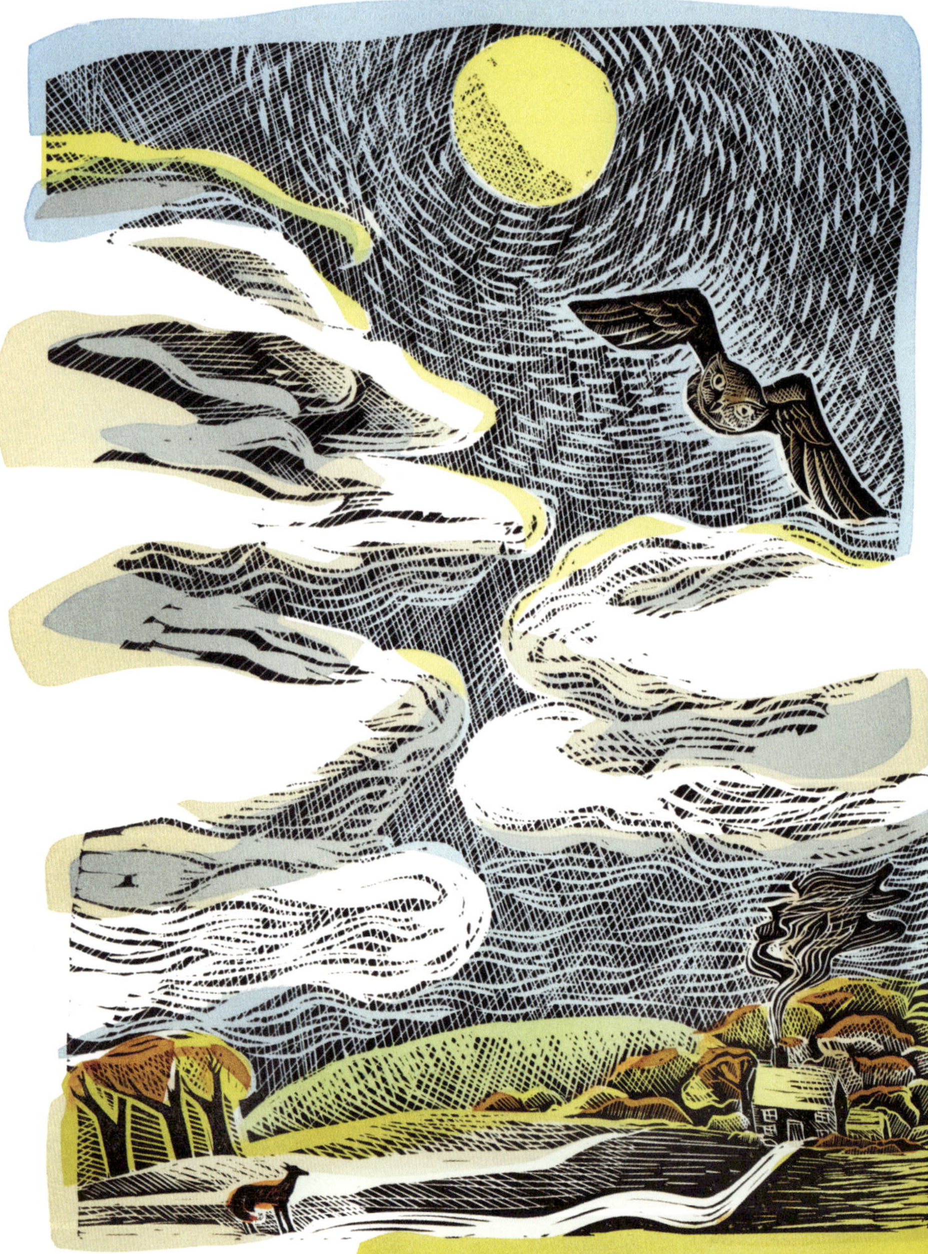

When I was working on the illustrated version of Isabella Tree's book *Wilding: How to Bring Wildlife Back*, I was given accommodation in a small woodland bothy. It was set in a small spinney of oak and beech trees with a pond at its edge. It was the perfect place to listen to the hooting of owls at night and, in the morning, watch foxes on the prowl around the pond looking for their breakfast.

Opposite:
Autumn Flight
(Linocut and silkscreen)

Nightjars are quite a rare sight in the UK. They are present in our locality, but I have never seen one. The place I have seen them is Costa Rica, where the days are short: by 6.30 p.m., night falls and the wildlife changes. Walking back from dinner along a woodland track, the ground was littered with nightjars. I moved my torch across the leafy ground and up rose a whirling mass of birds. Not just one nightjar but tens of them, spinning off into the night to hunt for moths and other insects.

Opposite:
Autumn Nightjar
(Linocut and silkscreen)

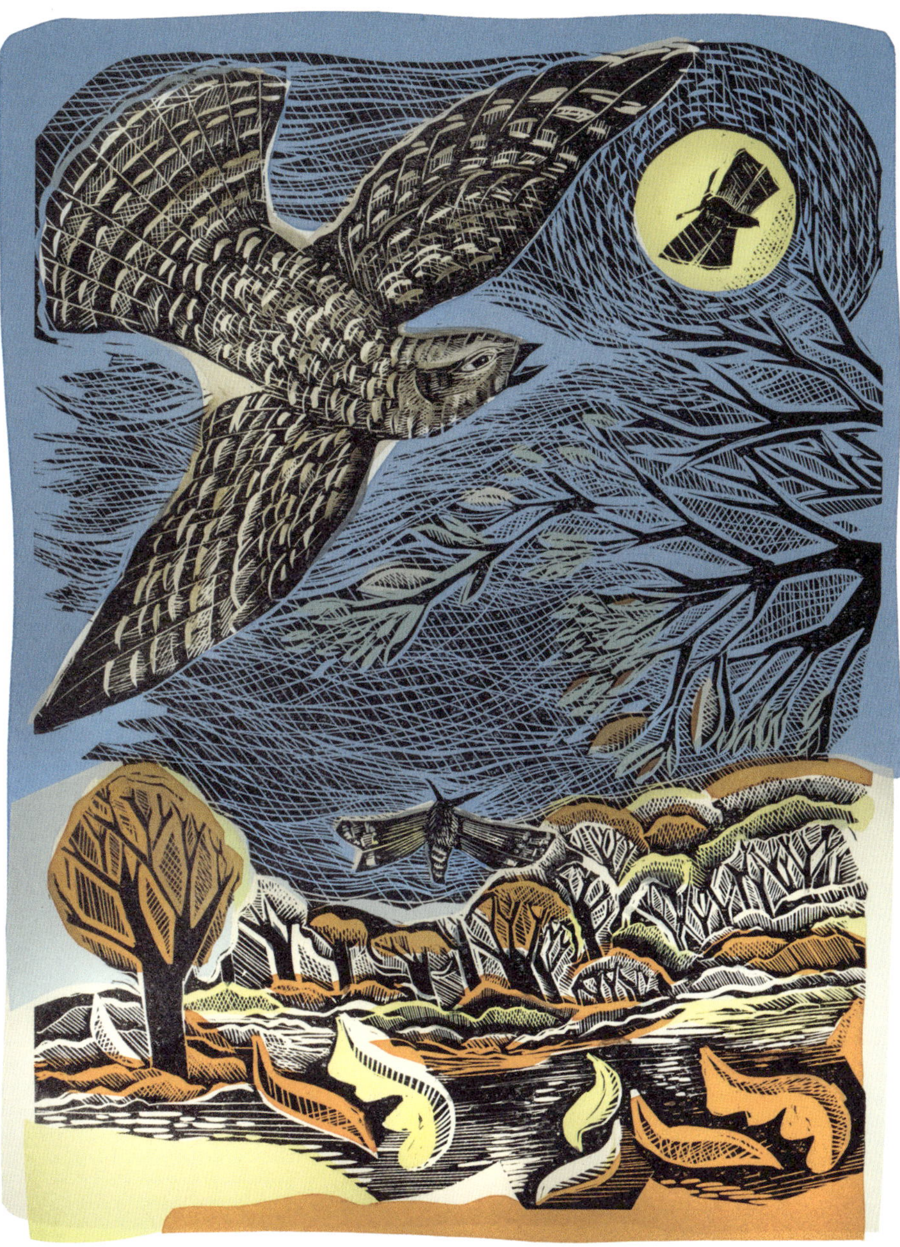

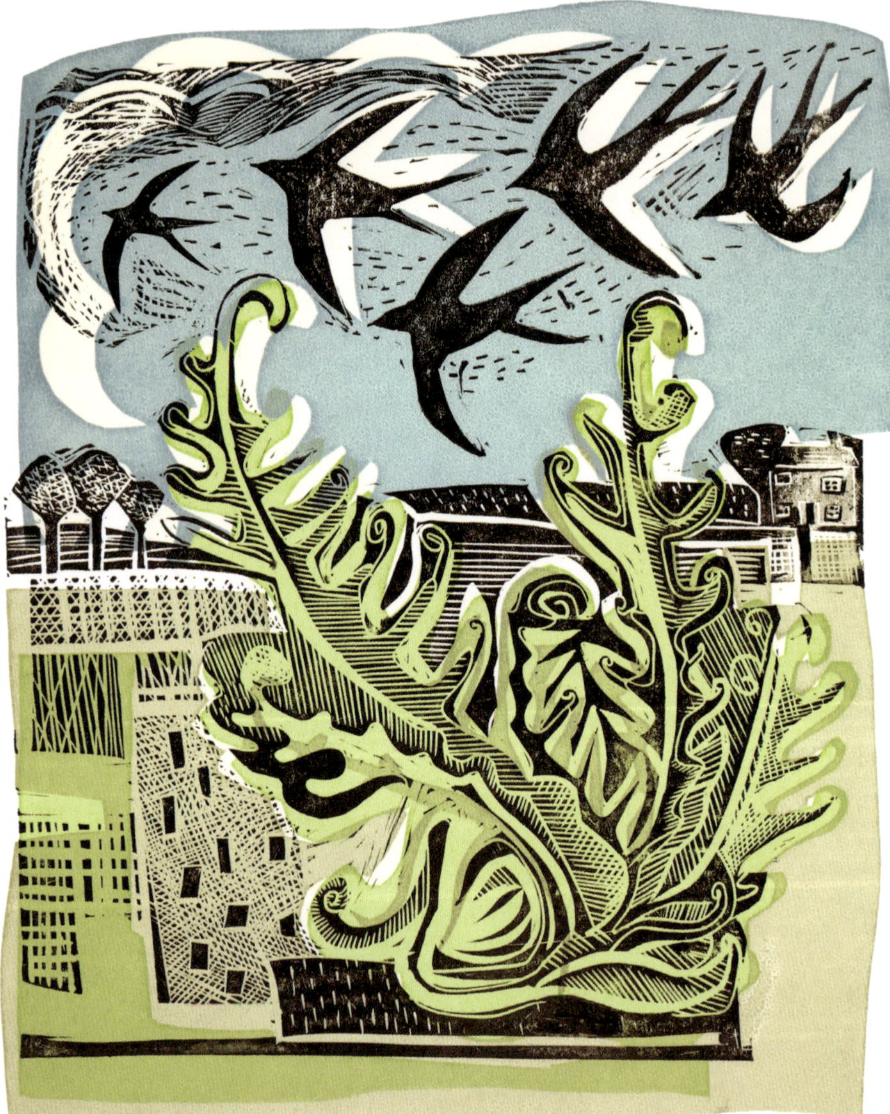

In the shady parts of my garden, ferns grow. In the springtime, the ferns unfurl their tight, rounded, bundled leaves into rich green fingers. By the autumn, these same leaves are starting to go brown at the edges. This seems to be at the same time that the swallows gather to leave. Groups of swallows sit in great flocks on the electric wires that are behind my studio. Together with the ferns, they are markers that the summer has gone; that one season has finished and another is about to begin.

Opposite:
Ferns
(Linocut and silkscreen)

Yellowhammers can be seen in our village throughout the year. In the autumn when the breeding season has passed, their plumage will be less vibrant. The bright yellow of their head and neck fades to a softer mustard colour, making them a little trickier to spot. I usually see them when I am out walking the dog. They top the hedgerows and gather in larger groups in the fields, often accompanied by twites and linnets.

Opposite:
Yellowhammer
(Wood engraving)

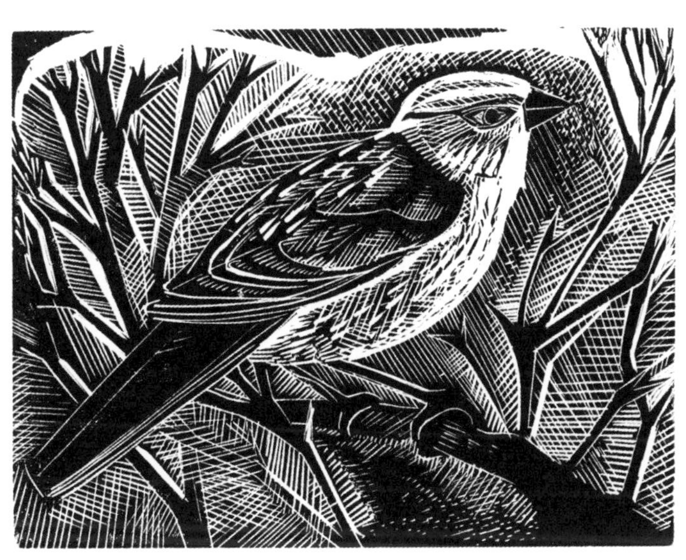

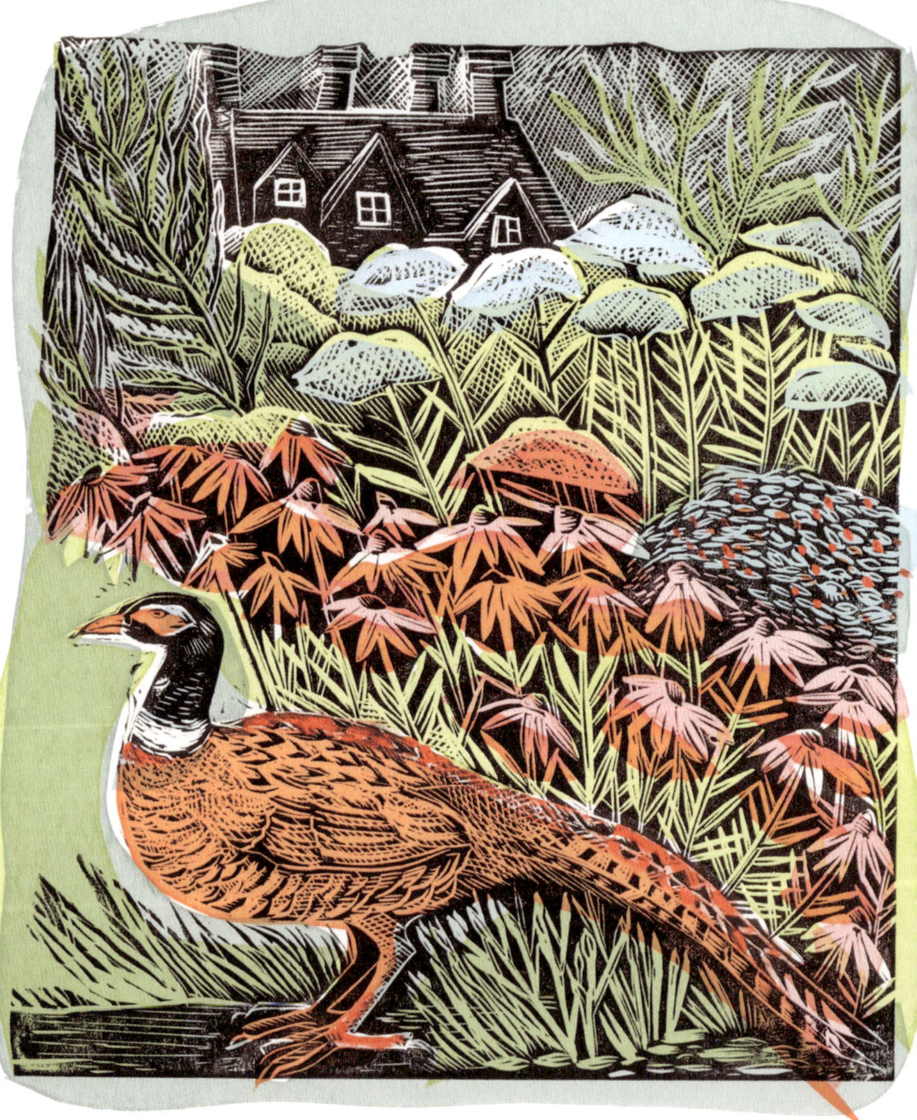

Pheasants are a common bird and, of course, they are not native to this country. I know they can bring a very destructive element to nature, but they are beautiful. The male birds in their fine bronze plumage always seem to appear in our lanes when the light is fading. The light exaggerates their colour so that they seem to glow.

Opposite:
Pheasant
(Linocut and silkscreen)

This print was drawn from childhood memories. I was born in Stoke-on-Trent and spent the first part of my early childhood in the village of Checkley, Staffordshire. This was my home till about the age of five, but I remember the garden most vividly. My mother was a great gardener and she loved red hot pokers; so did the chickens that weaved through them, seeking shade from the heat of the midday sun.

Opposite:
Chicken and Red Hot Pokers
(Linocut and silkscreen)

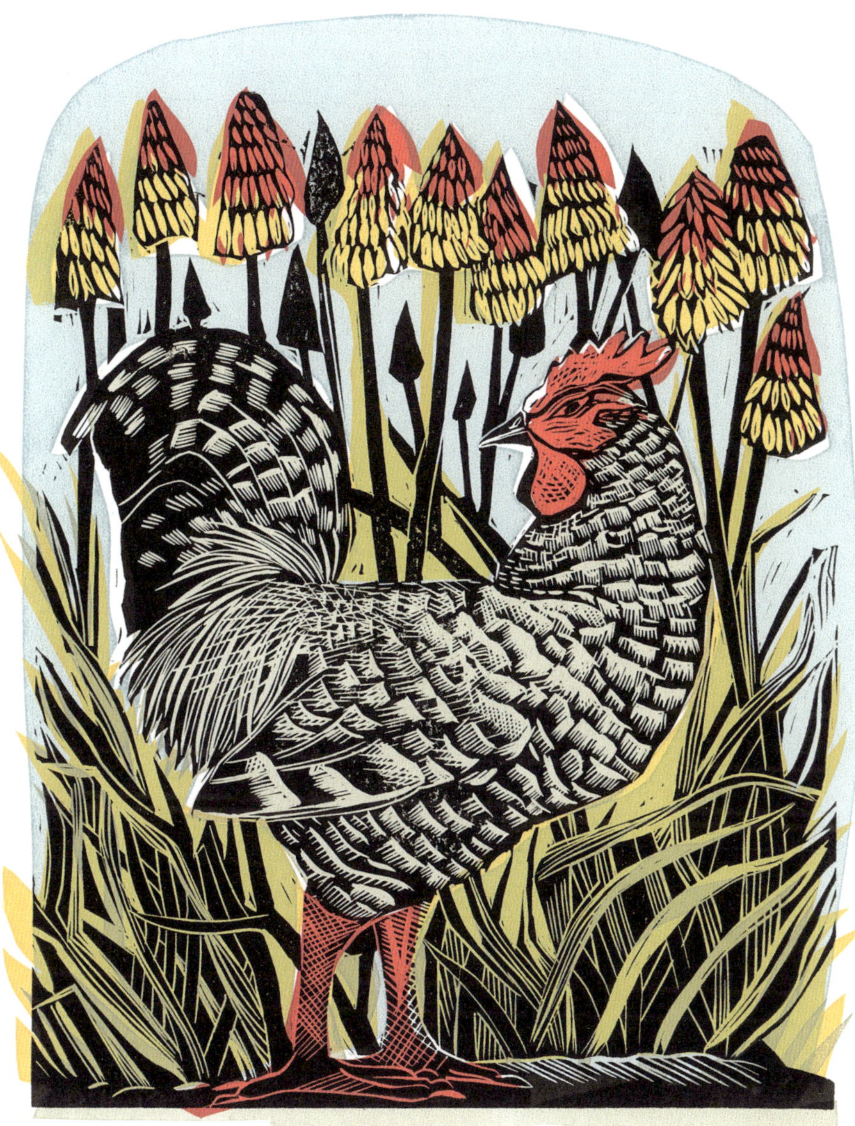

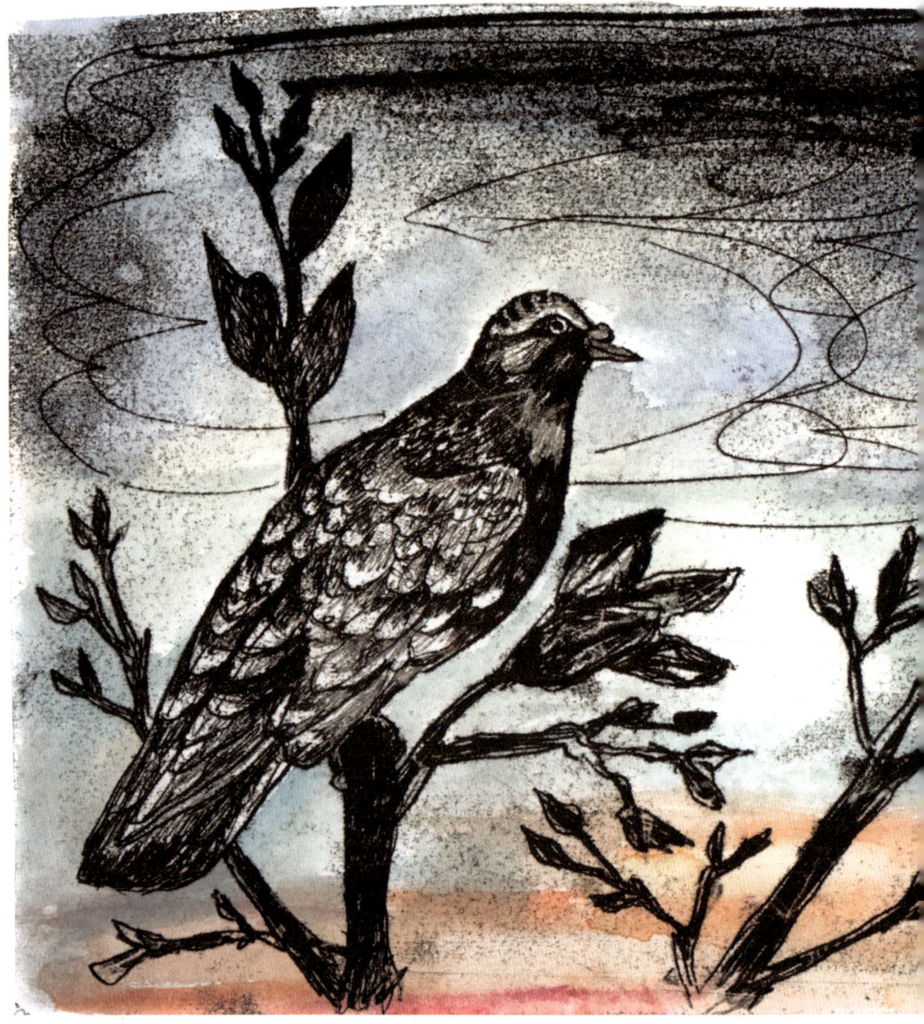

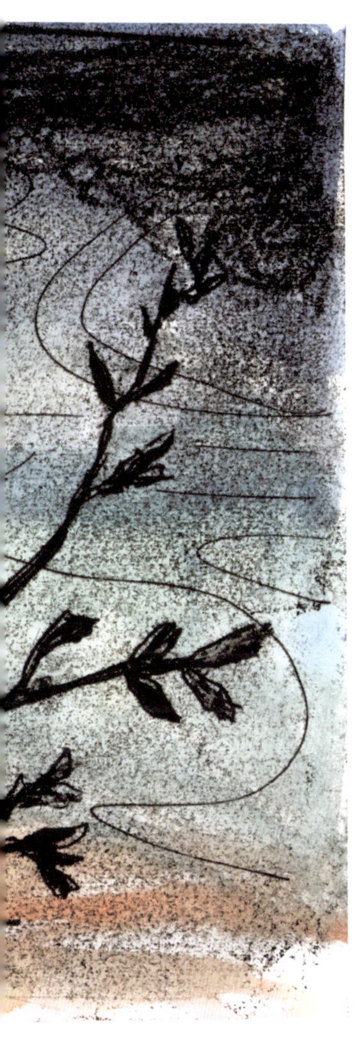

On a cloudless evening when the day's light is nearly gone, the sky can become a luminous backdrop for nature. Birds become silhouettes against delicate hues of pinks, oranges, greys and blues.

Opposite:
Fading Light
(Monoprint)

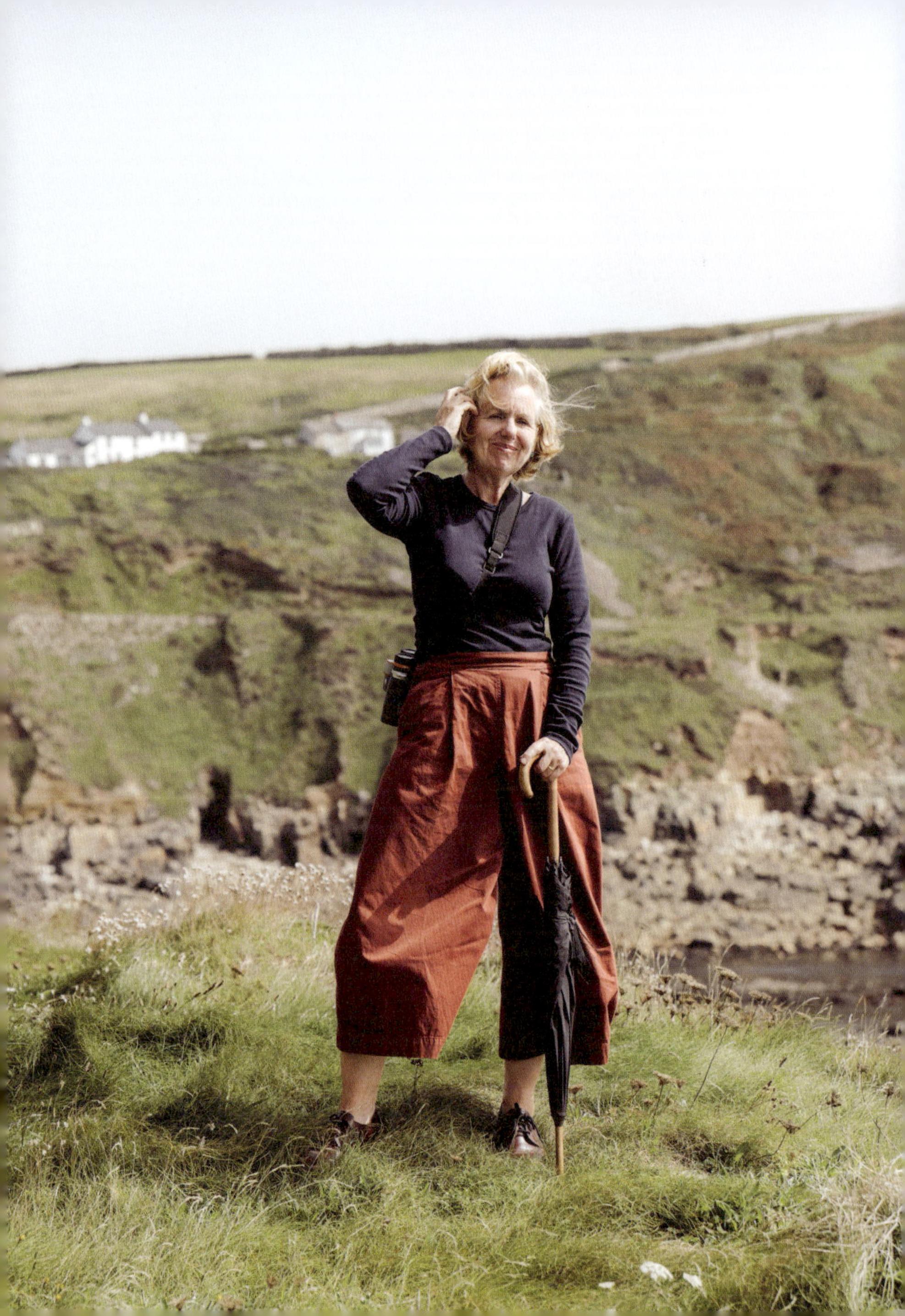

About the Author

ANGELA HARDING lives in the small county of Rutland and works out of the studio at the bottom of her garden in the village of Wing.

Angela has worked on the covers for a number of books, including P. D. James, Ted Hughes, Katya Balen and James Rebanks. Her children's book *RSPB Birds* by Miranda Krestovnikoff was longlisted for the Klaus Flugge Prize. Her most recent children's book, *Wilding*, by Isabella Tree, was shortlisted for the 2024 Wainwright Prize for Children's Writing on Nature and Conservation. Other recent publications include *Blossomise* by Simon Armitage, a *Sunday Times* bestseller.

Angela has written and illustrated three books published by Little, Brown: *A Year Unfolding*, *Wild Light* and *Still Waters & Wild Waves.*

Angela's unique and distinct style has become instantly recognisable to nature lovers and book lovers alike. Her fans flock to buy her merchandise, including calendars, cards, tea towels, tote bags and jigsaws.

She was the 2024 artist for the 'Books Are My Bag' tote bag, celebrating independent bookshops across the UK and Ireland.

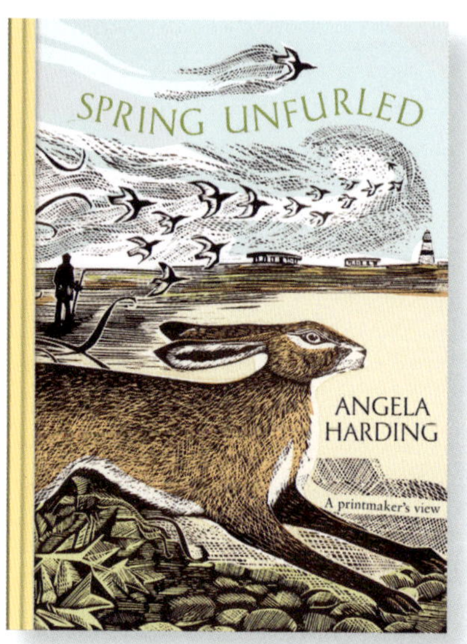

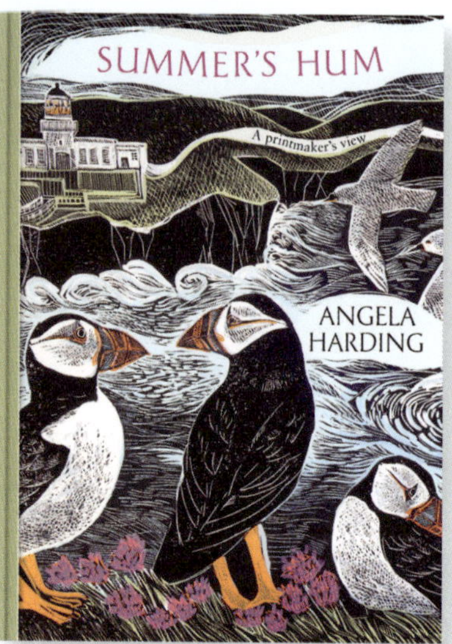

Collect the full Seasonal Quartet series

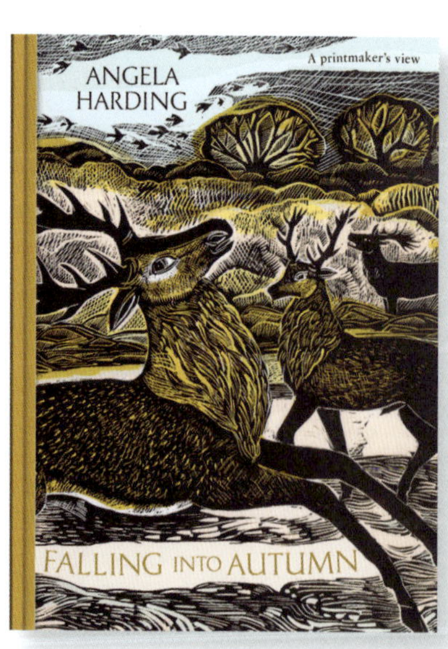

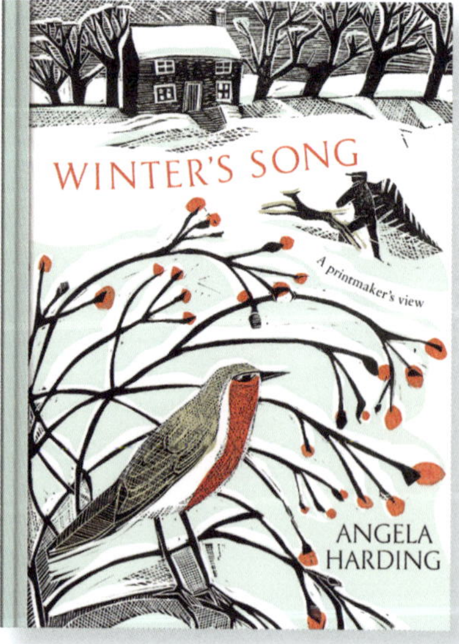

If you enjoyed
Falling into Autumn,
why not explore
Angela's other
books with
Little, Brown

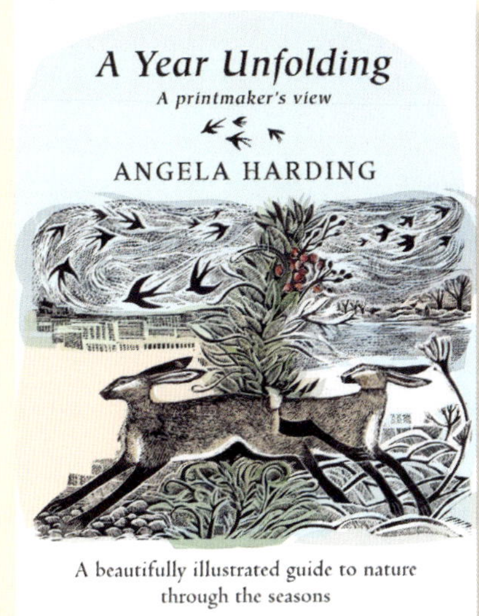

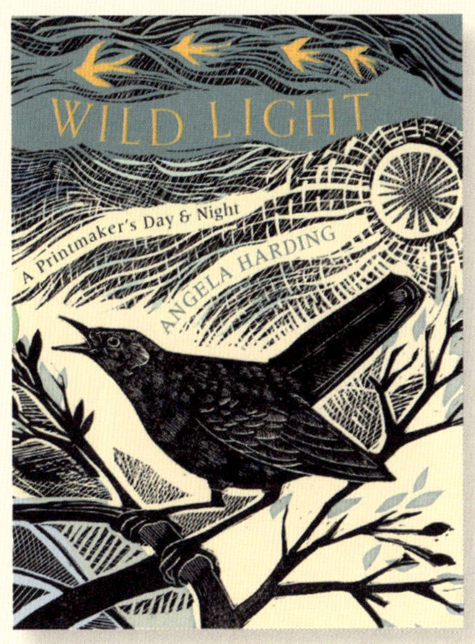

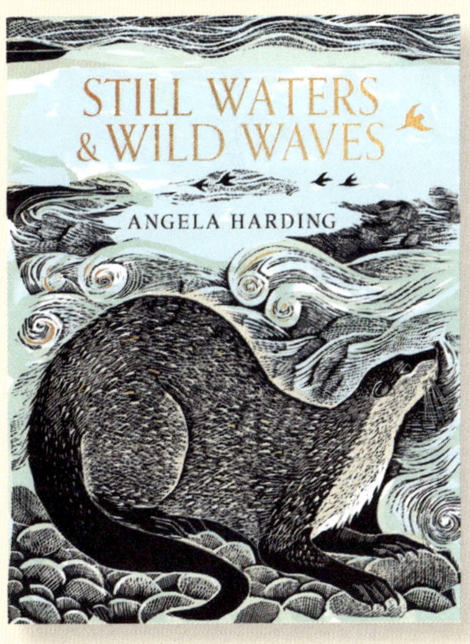

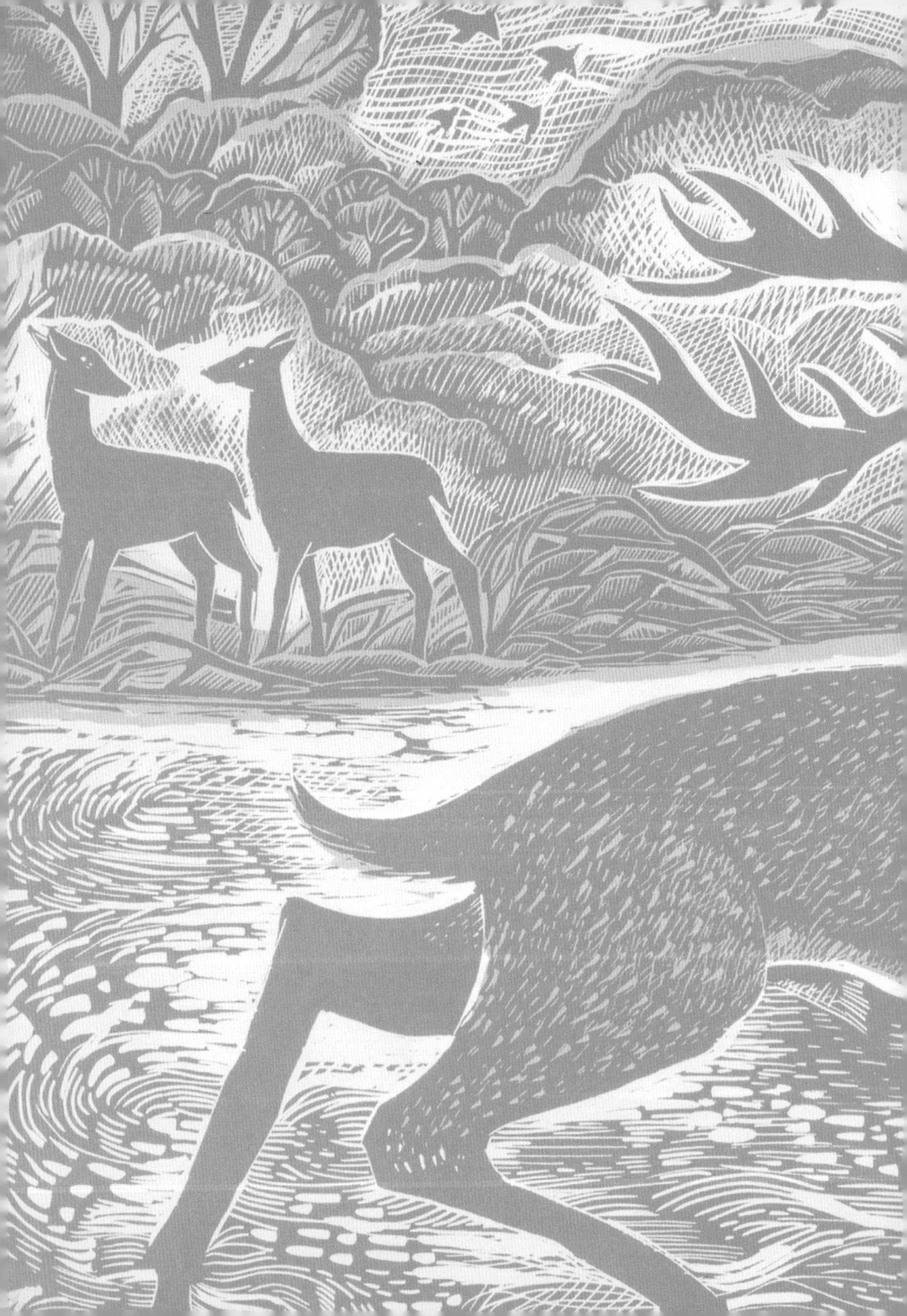